ALCHEMY

FROM

ASHES

PRAISE FOR *ALCHEMY FROM ASHES*

"Life after fifty can be full of uncertainty and a metamorphosis of transformation, if we are willing. In *Alchemy From Ashes* we experience the power of pain, loss, love, acceptance, and the power of alchemy."

—*Chip Conley, Founder of MEA and* New York Times
Bestselling Author of Learning to Love Midlife

"We can all identify with Kevin's story in some way. A story of strength, hope, resilience and transformation, *Alchemy from Ashes* provides insights that will help others wherever they are on their journeys. Articulately and beautifully crafted, his words share the power within each of us to provide life changing support – and sometimes life saving support – with others. Commonality, empathy, respect – Kevin's story illustrates that how we treat each other matters and that we all can make a difference. "

—*Dr. Patricia Newman, Child Psychologist &
Executive Director/Founder RESPECT*

"This book is a refreshing and emotional journey through 'becoming' in a world full of bigotry. No matter the prison we may live in, caused by prejudice and judgments, this book is a testimony that an authentic life is possible!"

—*Katie Jensen, MS LMHP*

ALCHEMY FROM ASHES

BRINGING MY SHATTERED FAITH,
MENTAL HEALTH, AND SEXUALITY
INTO WHOLENESS

KEVIN HUTCHISON

**Alchemy From Ashes: Bringing My Shattered Faith,
Mental Health, and Sexuality Into Wholeness**
Published by Windsor Sunrise Press, LLC
Omaha, NE

ISBN: 979-8-9985484-1-3

BIOGRAPHY & AUTOBIOGRAPHY / Memoirs

Cover and interior design by Ian Hutchison and Rachel Valliere,
Printed Page Studios, copyright owned by Kevin Hutchison

This book is not offering clinical or professional advice, and should
be viewed solely as the author's personal reflection and story.
The author and the publisher do not assume responsibility
or liability for the actions or decisions of the reader.

The stories shared in this book are based on the author's truth and memory.
While others may have various perspectives, memory is subjective based
on the person and their individual recall. This book contains themes
involving serious mental health topics including suicide. If you or someone
you know is in crisis, please call or text the Suicide Crisis Hotline at
988 or the Boys Town Crisis Services and Helpline at 800-448-3000.

QUANTITY PURCHASES: Schools, companies, professional groups,
clubs, and other organizations may qualify for special terms when
ordering quantities of this title. For information, visit (website).

This chronicle of my journey is dedicated to my guardian angel, Grandpa Gene. He was a role model of love, acceptance, and kindness to a traumatized youth—me—in this life. Grandpa Gene, thank you for watching over me and continuing to guide me.

"For He will give His angels charge concerning you, to guard you in all your ways."

PSALM 91:11 - 12

CONTENTS

PREFACE

"Just keep swimming, just keep swimming."

I never knew Dory's famous line from Pixar's *Finding Nemo* would become the mantra for my tumultuous journey toward the rebirth of my faith, mental health, and sexuality. But it did. The highlights and lowlights from my journey are included in the following pages.

My story is one of true alchemy. Alchemy, according to the *Webster's New World College Dictionary*, is defined as "a power or process of changing one thing into another, especially a seemingly miraculous power or process of changing a thing into something better." I chose this title because the trials, tribulations, losses, and enlightenment I experienced, and eventually embraced, forged my soul and life into something I never dreamed existed for me. A life where I am experiencing contentment, happiness, joy, self-love and acceptance.

As my journey unfolds on the following pages, it moves forward in a chronological fashion, with reflections back and forth in time to the people, places, and events that shaped a deep foundation of guilt, shame, and fear, as well as to moments of escape and solace amid the turbulence of my life. It also shares reflections on how perseverance, even when I did not feel it within myself, showed up in various forms to keep me moving forward.

My higher power, God, has always been a part of my life and belief system. I believe God is a beautifully melded gathering of all the masculine, the feminine, the paternal, and the maternal qualities and traits that exist in creation. Understanding the true loving, caring, and unconditional acceptance of the father heart of God was particularly a struggle for me. Our higher power seems to show up exactly when and how we need to experience Him, Her, or Them. Consequently, I always internally referred to God as He, even though I acknowledge and embrace all the other components. Reflecting on this wrestling match with God, and for ease of readership, I chose to refer to God as "He" in my story.

Come along with me on my journey, and, if you need to hear it as I did: "Just keep swimming." I have learned to keep moving, even if just barely, incrementally, and I encourage you to do the same.

CHAPTER 1

A Starry Night

THERE IS NOTHING LIKE a warm summer night in the heart of Chicago.

That's where I found myself in June of 2011, after spending the morning and afternoon working an international trade-show at McCormick Place with one of my firm's largest clients. The day had been full of excitement, learning, networking, and soaking in the sights and sounds of people from all over the globe. Then I'd topped it off with a fun client dinner.

After cocktails, friendly banter, debriefing, and a delicious meal, I wasn't quite ready to turn in for the evening. I draw a great deal of energy from being with others, and I was still feeling euphoric over my day. When I returned to my room, with its magnificent view of downtown, I was happy and satisfied, yet the city was still calling to me to come back out and play. I felt like Aladdin looking into the cave of wonders—the lights, people, bustling sidewalks and even the busy traffic all beckoned, inviting me into a new adventure. I felt excited and also a little unsettled as I asked myself, *bedtime or a walk?*

A walk won out.

I was still dressed up and feeling curious about the city and the people. While I then lived in Omaha, Nebraska, I had lived in or commuted to New York City for a number of years, so I was familiar with and drawn to the vibes, scents, and late nights of an urban center. Somehow, I always felt misplaced in Omaha and often had a sense of "wanderlust." I craved the fashion, coffee shops, late-night bars with live music, and energy that pulsed through the veins of larger cities. It seemed to be an invitation, creating a sense of acceptance and belonging that I desperately, and secretly, desired.

Having made my decision, I launched out from the high-rise hotel with the intention of walking for an hour or so, before returning to crash in my room.

There was a charged feeling in the air. Not just from the space around me, but also because of where I was in my life. I was fifty years old, and my youngest was just about to leave the house, making my wife and me "empty nesters." I knew change was coming.

As I headed along Michigan Avenue, light perspiration forming on my face and neck from the warm, humid air, I had a titillating sense of adventure. The sights and sounds of the city pushed me forward with exhilaration.

I looked up, noting the lights of skyscrapers along with the brightness of the stars. It was breathtaking. There were also people all around me—out walking, ducking into restaurants, bars, and music venues. I have a core belief there is something good or beautiful in every living being, even if sometimes you must take detours and dig deeper to find the treasure that hides within. And this belief leads me to really enjoy being with people and surrounded by them.

On this particular night, there was so much to take in. I was grateful to be there experiencing all of it.

I entered a crosswalk off E. Ontario Street and began to cross with the crowd. As my crossing was almost complete, I noticed someone out of the corner of my left eye.

He stood out from the people around him—a handsome man wearing shorts, a fitted short-sleeve Polo shirt, and Ed Hardy Converse tennis shoes. I turned my gaze just enough to notice he also glanced at me.

My first instinct was to keep walking, as I was already across the street; however, butterflies filled my stomach, I was light-headed and experiencing thoughts and sensations I hadn't felt for years. So, I made an out-of-character and abrupt turn-around. I was stuck in a crowd, but I was able to make my way back where I originally started to cross. I looked up and there he was, waiting for me. Standing under the blinking "Don't Walk" sign with a slight smile on his face and a twinkle in his eyes.

As cliché and crazy as it may sound, it felt like the scene from *Sleepless in Seattle,* when Tom Hanks crosses the busy road to meet Meg Ryan in the middle and they both stand there in a daze, only able to say "hello."

I felt magic as I introduced myself and he did likewise.

His name was John. And when I asked him if he wanted to go somewhere, have a drink, and talk...he said yes.

What am I doing? I asked myself.

This was new to me, and I began to (briefly) second guess myself before settling into the thought, *a conversation won't hurt anything*.

We headed down E. Ontario, walking and talking, until we saw a sign for the Redhead Piano Bar. The crowds of people, loud music, and fun atmosphere looked safe and inviting. John agreed, and we waited in line until we eventually made it to the bouncer, dressed in a suit. He informed John that although his unique and cool shoes were amazing, dress shoes were required. He next offered him a pair of black dress shoes to borrow, and John grimaced at the thought of wearing someone else's shoes without socks. We both laughed and decided to find another, less formal, option for our conversation.

We kept walking.

John's company, and the nighttime sights and smells around me, intrigued me and buoyed me to keep moving forward. I suddenly felt like I was walking on air, floating down the street with this handsome, vivacious, and interesting soul. He was from a large city a few thousand miles away and had an alluring accent to top it off!

We eventually stepped into Pops for Champagne, a champagne bar. As we entered, the bustle of the patrons, and the smell of carbonated wines and antipasto appetizers filled the air. The main bar area was packed, so we found a table toward the back.

John and I sat across from each other and started getting to know each other over a glass of chardonnay.

We talked about our jobs, partners, and families, and I was immediately struck by our similarities and situations. Like me, he felt strong loyalty to his loved ones and his company. He was also just coming out of a long-term relationship (with a man) and settling into life on his own again, and while I wasn't leaving my marriage at that time, the insecurities and fears he shared around the life change resonated with me.

Somewhere amid the conversation, our arms, which had been resting on the table, touched and slightly brushed together. I felt electricity suddenly pulse through my veins, and I was overwhelmed with giddiness and infatuation—not one bit of it from the alcohol. I could see John was genuinely interested in listening to me, and I felt seen, heard, and accepted, maybe for the first time ever. There were no awkward pauses, no grasping for conversation. Everything flowed naturally, and we lost track of time. We enjoyed a couple of drinks before wrapping up our conversation. He offered to walk me back to my hotel so we could continue talking.

As we walked back to my hotel, I didn't want our time to end. I felt a growing warm, burning sensation on my face and neck—anxiety, nerves, paranoia, and fear. Beads of sweat formed on my brow.

I asked him if he would like to come up to my room.

John looked me in the eyes, with a half-smile on his face, and said yes.

Once in my room, we stood in front of the large wall-length window overlooking downtown Chicago from the twenty-eighth floor. The city lights and stars in the sky seemed to paint the perfect backdrop for this chance meeting of two kindred souls who'd collided at a crosswalk. And now here we were. I was with someone I really did not know, and yet, I felt like I had always known him.

I felt lightheaded from the endorphin rush, tingling all over at the realization I was on the precipice of one of the biggest decisions of my life. As I stood there looking into his eyes, my world passed before my eyes. I saw my wife, my religious beliefs, my family, really everything—and I almost audibly heard a voice in my head. *You are about to make a decision that will forever change the course of your life. Nothing will ever be the same.*

I mentally acknowledged it. I accepted it. And then I made the conscious choice to move forward.

John reached over and slowly unbuttoned my dress shirt, and I in turn slipped his pastel Polo shirt over his head. We locked eyes and then held each other in silence while staring out the window at the enchanting and calming view. My heart was pounding, and the adrenalin flowing, as a lifetime of repression engulfed me. At the same time, there was stillness and peace in being held tightly by this strong man. Such a duality of feelings, and yet, they all coexisted within me and felt right.

In the span of the next few hours, I fell hard for him—his sense of humor, handsomeness, kindness, and ability to read me. I was deeply touched by his acceptance of my awkwardness and refusal to go any further than simply being close to one another. He seemed to understand my boundaries and reservations, and he appeared to simply enjoy being with me. I had been faithful to my wife over the years. Flirtations and conversations occurred with others; however, I had vowed to never let it go further. John, though, touched a piece of my heart that no one else had for a very long time. The red warning light was flashing in my mind and yet, I sensed he would be a potential friend and confidant, far more than a one-night stand. The sense that fate had stepped into my life and perhaps this wasn't a "chance meeting," darted through my mind.

Looking back, although I knew I was changing the course of my life, I had no idea how resounding that decision and change would be. Like ripples from a rock tossed in a pond, the ripples lasted for days, months, and years.

They still continue today.

Later I would call this encounter and its subsequent ripples my "awakening."

I think we all have at least one awakening in our lives. It's a time when everything intersects—the good, the bad, the beautiful, and the ugly, and the result is a change to our course of action. My awakening put me at a crossroads in life where I felt I couldn't go backward, and yet—I couldn't quite go forward either.

My initial reaction to what had happened was joy. I knew something deep within me had finally been unlocked, touched, and set free. It was the beginning of a revelation of who I was, and I was setting myself on a path to try to figure it out. When I first returned home from my trip, I felt happy, with an aura of a lovesick puppy. My joy, passion, and optimism about where this might go pushed me forward for a long time. Simultaneously, the weight of the secret, the reality that I had begun to let my sexuality out of the bag, started to weigh on my heart and mind. The heaviness only increased over time, as I trusted no one with this secret. I believed it could destroy me if I didn't handle it just right—and yet, I didn't know how to handle it. This was unchartered territory. Over time, sadness, anger, and grief began to outweigh the other emotions. I went through an affair grief cycle which, as The Gottman Institute defines it, includes denial, anger, bargaining, depression, acceptance, and post-traumatic stress disorder (PTSD). This grief cycle, similar to what anyone experiencing loss in their life goes through, can be particularly brutal for the betrayed, and in my case, for me, as the betrayer.

A large portion of my grief came from violating the vows and parameters I'd spent my whole life maintaining. Whether they were related to marriage, faith, or the secrecy and taboo around my sexuality, they formed a black and white box that served as an underground electric fence that kept me in line—or in a safe place, as I then thought. I would later learn, through therapy, that my rigid thinking and inability to see the dialectic in things was a major source of my growing anxiety and depression, an indicator of my declining mental health. My mind would focus on right and wrong and good and bad, and this singular focus in thinking was slowly suffocating me, instead of setting me free.

I asked myself *how could I live a life that was joyous, happy, and free? Was it even possible for me?* The question was too big for me, too heavy, and the dark fingers of hopelessness began to sink into my brain. I tried not to let the dark thoughts in. Instead, I focused on my relationship with John, obsessed over it in fact. I desperately desired a deep relationship with him, yet it wasn't fully attainable. He lived thousands of miles away, and I certainly couldn't cross that territory and join him.

Then I began to question *have I been here before?* Living with one foot in and one foot out, always trying to straddle the middle or neutral ground. In this case: having an incredible long-distance connection to John, yet not risking a continued physical relationship with him. As much as I thought I had wanted to stand out, be seen, be heard, be accepted, I realized I often chose to live in the abyss of the middle. And it was coming to feel like bland vanilla ice cream, with no distinct flavor or texture of its own. I learned that when you live in the middle for too long, you die, either emotionally, spiritually, or physically—or from a combination of all three.

Eventually I collapsed, emotionally and spiritually, and came very close to dying physically as well. I wasn't ready to face any of it, though, so I retreated to self-preservation.

At the time, that meant keeping what had happened a secret.

Keeping it buried didn't really seem that bad. Keeping secrets was one thing I was really good at, so it didn't seem like such a big deal. After all, I didn't want to hurt anyone, so secrecy seemed the best option.

Meanwhile, I continued a long-distance phone relationship with John. Although I questioned (and suffered with) the middle ground of it, the distance also allowed us to have long, meaningful conversations with each other with no expectations. I discovered further commonalities in personality traits, love of family, friends, and sadness and regret over our current relationships with our partners (or in his case, his prior partner). I also learned about, and admired him, for our differences. He loved sports, the outdoors, and enjoyed kayaking and biking.

He was a deep, intricate, and interesting person, and I kept thinking how he was someone my children would like and enjoy getting to know. I often fantasized about introducing them. As we continued talking, I grew deeper in love with him, as a friend. I also valued and respected the patience and wisdom he offered in listening to me, as I often cried over my situation, emotions spewing like Mount Vesuvius. I had not been through much therapy yet, and the strength of my emotions made me feel like a teenager. They controlled me at times, as I did not know how to process them appropriately, nor did I know how to build healthy relationships.

Secrets and codependency were the drugs that helped me cope, and oh, I loved them both. I was a product of a secretive and traumatic childhood, and it built a foundation for my life. Now, the foundation was cracked, and that crack was ever widening,

Around this time, I began having an extra glass or two of wine to settle my nerves and numb the emotional pain. This initiated a pattern of coping that would only get worse and exacerbate my emotional insecurities and anxiety. All of this became just another secret to keep.

By outward appearances, I appeared successful and doing fine. I held a prominent position in a global advertising agency, and I had a beautiful wife, a house in the suburbs, and three children pursuing life with passion. That was the American dream, right? And yet, here I was after all these years, suppressing my sexuality, feeling lost, alone, and grappling with deep grief and a myriad of other emotions and feelings.

My joy was eroding, the secrets were feeling heavier, and fear was building. My old ways of thinking were not giving me answers, and I began asking myself, *how did I get here and how do I get out?*

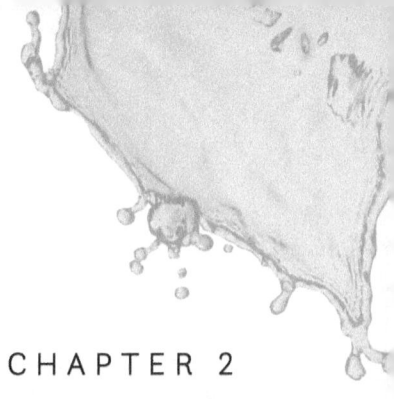

CHAPTER 2

Pandora's Box of Fear and Secrets

"If a fear cannot be articulated, it can't be conquered."

—Stephen King, Salem's Lot

WHEN I FIRST READ Stephen King's novel *Salem's Lot* as a sixth-grade kid, it terrified me.

The book tells the story of a town overtaken by vampires who come calling for their victims in the night while they are sleeping, waking them by scratching on the windows. In my life, I had experienced my own vampires, and because of it, I always felt there was someone or something scratching on my window, trying to get in—or maybe trying to take something away. As I mentioned, secrets and fear defined me from an early age, and they continued to be strong, hurricane forces blowing into my adult life.

Looking back, where did fear and secrecy take root? I don't know that I can pinpoint when exactly it started, because I feel like I always carried fear with me. There was, though, a

Titanic of experiences, which happened when I was eleven years old. At this age, I was an insecure, overweight, glasses-wearing, acne-infested pre-teen. I struggled in school to fit in—the last one picked for the team in PE, getting called a "fag," and getting my books dumped daily. Things at home, where I lived with my parents, my older sister, and my little mixed breed dog, Ginny, were also hard. My mother had been sick for many years.

One morning, before school, my dad told me she would be gone when I got home from school. He was sending her to a mental hospital, where they would help her get better, he said.

I wanted her to get better. Even if her behavior was erratic and cruel at times, I loved her and I knew she loved me.

I remember when I was in elementary school, and she took me back-to-school shopping at JC Penney. We didn't have a lot of money, and my dad kept a tight budget, so that day we were browsing for a minimal number of practical items I needed—some husky-size jeans and utilitarian, plain shirts. Unfortunately for my mom, my attraction to a dramatic and more flamboyant style of clothing kicked in. Walking around the corner of the clothing aisle, I spied an incredible blue and white floral shirt, with billowing sleeves and a navy-blue fringed suede vest. It felt like finding buried treasure! I was smitten, totally in love with this David Cassidy, Partridge Family style and look. Nothing else would do. I pleaded with my mom to buy it. Initially she said no, knowing what would happen when my dad found out. He would be furious, as it was not in the budget, it wasn't practical, and it wasn't masculine. It certainly wasn't the plaid shirt he was hoping to see come out of the bag. Yet eventually, she relented and made my night. I was over the moon with happiness and joy. Those emotions were soon squelched by my dad's response and, even more, by my classmates, the following day. Feeling stupid, silly, rejected, and ashamed of myself and my choice, I asked myself, *what was I thinking?* I gave the shirt to my sister, and I hung the vest in my closet, where I looked at it longingly every day. However, I will never forget my sweet mother's kindness and bravery in attempting to let me be me.

I didn't want her sent away.

When I walked home after school that day, it was warm and sunny, and the birds were singing. Yet, I was feeling anxious and worried as I made my way, perspiring, down our suburban, tree-lined street. When I walked through the front door of our small ranch house, I smelled grease and french fries. I saw my sister and her boyfriend sitting at the kitchen table eating Burger King, and my dad pacing in the living room, tension hanging thick in the air. I was shocked, confused, and angry. How could they sit there so calmly eating, when our world was about to be turned upside down? I could feel the panic and sense of helplessness building in my head and chest. It seemed as if I might burst. Beads of sweat broke out on my forehead and my underarms were soaked. My dad quickly told me my mom was locked in their bedroom—they were late coming to get her, but would be there at any moment. I was suddenly paralyzed. My head began to pound, and fear, anger, and protectiveness pumped through my veins. My dad sent me to my room, where I tearfully leaned against the wall, peering out the window. It was only a few minutes before an ominous, big black sedan with tinted windows pulled into the driveway. Usually, I would have associated this type of car with a limousine with someone famous inside. Instead, this vehicle felt dark, evil, and foreboding. It was about to swallow my mother up, and I wasn't sure if she would ever return.

Two men in suits came into our house and proceeded to the bedroom. My mother did not want to go with them. She screamed for help, but when threatened with a straitjacket, she somewhat cooperated as they twisted her arms behind her back, treating her like a wild animal that had to be controlled. She begged me to help her, calling my name, and asking me to make them stop, saying she wanted to stay home. My face was red, burning, as tears rolled down my cheeks. My stomach ached, and I felt helpless and afraid. Once the door shut and the black sedan pulled away, I lay on my bed, sobbing, wondering if life would ever be the same again—and if my mother would ever return to our house.

This became the biggest secret I ever had to keep. Because of the stigma of mental illness at the time, my dad instructed me to never tell anyone about my mom's mental breakdown. We lied to the neighbors, we lied to our friends about where she was, and we lied to my teachers about why I was missing school because I was making myself sick. We buried that secret deep down inside the vault of our very beings. Even after she came home, we did not talk about it, and acted like it was something that never happened, even though she returned an entirely different person.

My mother was institutionalized for a few weeks—I can't remember the exact length as it all blurred together. But I know I missed her so badly my stomach ached.

My dad sent me to stay for a week or two with his mother, my grandma, whom I loved. She tried to take my mind off things by playing dominoes with me, baking cookies, and taking me shopping, but I just wanted to go home and see my mom, to know she was okay. I was terrified thinking about what they might be doing to her, as I had heard my dad talking about electric shock treatments that were sometimes used.

A distraction was remembering the good memories with my mom. What she was like before the darkness overcame her. Yet still, I worried, and I worried, and I worried some more.

Eventually, my grandma drove me the couple of hours back home. It was time for my mom to come home.

I was filled with anxiety, excitement, and an overwhelming love for her. I walked to the store and bought her a single stem red carnation in a vase with a bow on it. I also wanted to decorate the house to let her know it was a happy and wonderful homecoming—that she had been missed, and she was loved. But my grandma had other ideas. She sat me down and instructed me there would be no decorations and no hoopla, as we did not want to agitate my mother or upset her in any way. She thought it best if we had a quiet homecoming with a simple meal.

My dad left to pick her up, and when they returned, she walked in the door dressed in a polyester pantsuit. I handed her my meager flower, and she hugged me tightly. She told me she had missed me and loved me. I cried. I had missed her terribly and I was so happy she was home. However, fear crouched behind my happiness.

As I looked at her, something was different. There was a vacantness in her eyes. Her voice was more monotone, and her movements slower. This would never change over the years. Later, I learned the medication used on her was like having a chemical lobotomy. My mother whom I had known— with all the good and the bad—was gone forever.

It would be six years before I told someone about her mental illness and what had happened—and much longer before I shared it again with anyone else. I believed if anyone found out, they would reject me (and God knows, I had already endured a great deal of bullying and rejection in my young life), not love me, and think there was something wrong with me and my family.

This experience solidified secrecy as one of my core values. It also bolstered my foundational desire and need for the approval of others—my need to make them happy and never upset them so that they wouldn't then hurt, reject, or dislike me. It would take years of therapy to turn this thinking around, and honestly, I still struggle with it at times, as it creeps back into my thinking.

Whenever there is a void in our lives, we seek to fill it, sometimes with things that are good for us, and other times with things that may not be so good. I've always related to the story of the children's book, *Are You My Mother?* By P.D. Eastman, where the bird continually seeks his mother and can't find her. Like the little bird—even once my mother had returned home—I looked up and didn't see her, I looked down and didn't see her, and then I determined, I must go and find a mother. I was constantly looking for role models; men, women, and families who would accept me, love me, and not abandon me. A few positive and significant ones come to mind, as being sent by a power greater than myself, to stand in the gap, and encourage me on my path. Most were women. I found several brave, intuitive, strong, kind, caring, compassionate, and empathetic women who were willing to stand in the gap. Although they knew they were not my mother, they knew, in essence, I needed them to be, and they provided nurturing and elements of wisdom, guidance, and encouragement along my way.

One of these was a creative and beautiful female soul in the form of my sixth-grade teacher, Ms. Woods, who entered my life at the time of my mother's breakdown and institution-alization. She taught creative arts, and brought the world to life in a sensory way like no one else had ever done for me. I was sad, depressed, confused, and tormented by being a secret keeper. Many of the other students thought she was a little out there, often wearing knickerbockers and clogs, but I was drawn to her like a fly to flypaper. Her Spidey-sense must have been going off, because she made room for me in her life and teaching in caring and uncommon ways. I loved her acting classes, and I quickly jumped into tryouts for various skits and one act plays. In addition, she taught me to ballroom dance in after-school sessions. Here I was, feeling like a sweaty, overweight, ugly, acne-infested, twelve-year-old, with a broken heart. She gave me rides home, once took me for a soda, and introduced me to her family. I had to get glasses while in her class, and she turned that experience from something I thought was awful into an amazing opportunity to see the world and nature's beauty in a whole new way, appreciating every color and every detail. Through her, I experienced, love, caring, validation, and belonging, at a time when I needed it most.

During my teen years, I also adopted a mom, or I think she adopted me. Ms. Blake was a neighbor, with seven children. I was good friends with one of her boys, so we spent a lot of time at their house, and I absolutely loved the chaotic contrast of their home to ours. We played kick-the-can in their backyard, and we kids would sit inside at night and talk with her, make no-bake peanut butter and oatmeal cookies, and popcorn with oodles of butter, while she was sewing or doing laundry. The smells of the house, the noise of the seven kids coming and going—slamming doors, talking, eating, and playing—filled my senses in a way my empty and lonely home could not. Often, I marveled at Ms. Blake's ability to be a mother to such a big family, with the amount of love and gentleness she expressed. Nothing seemed to rattle her; she appeared calm, cool, and collected most of the time. I always told her she was like Cinderella, a beautiful, kind person, mending, cooking, cleaning, and taking care of others—a comparison she always remembered and wrote about in a card for my mom's funeral several years ago. Cinderella made a difference in my young life. She accepted me, loved me, listened to me, fed me, and treated me like just another one of her little birds in her nest. Like my teacher, I think Cinderella sensed, "This boy needs a home!" And I always wished that I could have taken her to the ball.

My search was always on, just like the little bird. Fortunately, I also became part of another wonderful family in my pre-teen and teen years. They were like the families on television, and had fun together, went on trips together, and were accepting and loving. One boy was my age, and he had a younger brother who tagged along with us, too. I would go to the pool with them, go camping, have sleepovers on the pullout sofa at their house, and go out to eat with them. They also loved themed dinner nights. I remember my favorite was Chinese night, when his mom would make LA Choy Chow Mein (from a can!) with crunchy noodles, eggrolls, and fortune cookies. I thought they were the most fun, adventurous people I had ever met. I loved every minute, and when I woke up there after a sleepover to the sweet smell of pancakes, bacon frying, and scrambled eggs with cheese, I thought I was in heaven. I never, ever wanted to go home. They also had the most adorable dachshund who would squeal and bark, "I love you!" when you held a treat over her head. Because she was so amazing, my unending love affair with the dachshund breed began. The little Doxie symbolizes happy memories for me. It is a symbol of a family who took me in as another one of their boys—they gave me a place to belong.

Most of my surrogates were female; however, there was one very important male figure in my life. That man was my grandfather. In my teen years especially, I never knew I could love someone as much as I loved him. My mom's father, he was a farmer, tough, and tender. I have wonderful, fun, and adventurous memories of summer days on the farm, where he and my grandma lived in an old two-story farmhouse. They had no running water, no air conditioning (despite it being very hot in the southern Missouri summer), no neighbors in sight, and no indoor bathrooms. I had three cousins similar in age, and we had such fun running through the fields, chasing animals, watching fireflies and bats outside at night—and even going on adventures with the flashlight to the outhouse. The sounds after dark—cows, coyotes, and who knows what else—only solidified our belief in ghosts, werewolves, and other creatures of the night. And then, sweaty and tired, all of us cousins would crash on the floor, or pile in a bed in the attic, the sheets sticking to our bodies in the humidity, hearing scary noises in the wind as we drifted off to sleep.

My grandpa paid a little special attention to me, or at least I thought so. I think his intuition told him that I needed some love and a sense of direction and belonging in my life. I used to sit on the back porch with him at night after supper, and we would feed the meal scraps to the dogs and countless farm cats. As they all came to the porch to eat, we would sit, talk, and pet the creatures. He didn't hesitate to put a work-roughened hand on my shoulder, or hold my hand in his, as he taught me new things, like milking a cow.

My favorite lesson was when he taught me how to roll his cigarettes, using his own rolling papers and pure tobacco. I would smell the sweet and smoky aroma of the crushed tobacco leaves as I helped roll them into unfiltered cigarettes. That was our special time, just him, me, the dogs, and a myriad of cats, sitting outside laughing and talking, and just being boys. He always had time for me, and I never felt like a burden when I asked questions or wanted to go out in the fields with him. He and my grandma would write me letters and we were planning for me to spend my first whole summer on the farm when I was fifteen. We wrote about how we were going to go terrapin turtle hunting and frog fishing—he loved frog legs, and we planned to catch a bunch of them from his pond and cook them up special for supper one night while I was there. Unfortunately, the dreams, plans, and the summer on the farm never happened. My grandpa became gravely ill with cancer, an aggressive and fast form of it. He died right before the summer I would have spent there. I was heartbroken, and I do not think I had ever cried that hard previously. He was my one male role model that I looked up to. He was tough, tender, compassionate, loving, fun, and accepting—and within a short time of his diagnosis, he was gone forever. To this day, when I smell gardenias, I am triggered with his memory, because I associate the smell with the flowers at his funeral. Not only did he die, but a part of me did also—and my hopes and dreams for spending time with him, learning, growing, and receiving love. Little did I know, he would be watching over me and I would sense his presence again, many years ahead, like a guardian angel. I have a picture of him on my desk so I will never forget he was with me then, and he is with me now. While he has been gone for a long time now, I believe he is still with me and has watched over me all these years.

Looking back now, I wonder if my parents were ever jealous of some of my surrogate moms and dads. I was always looking up, looking down, looking all the way around, for someone or something to make me feel safe, at home, to take me in, and give me that sense of belonging. And I wasn't able to find it at home. My family always felt so disjointed and distant. My sister and I were seven years apart, and she already had one foot out of the house when my mom had her mental breakdown. We were two very separate children, trying to find their way. My dad worked nights, so he slept during the day and left for work when I was getting home from school. The feeling of connectedness was absent, both before and after my mom's health decline. I do, though, have memories from before the breakdown of my mom laughing, baking cookies, and making popcorn balls for me. She also used to take great pride in making fabulous teacher gifts for Christmas for my teachers—homemade candles, needlepoint pillows, and other thoughtful handmade items. As the darkness of her mental health settled in, all the fun and unique things slowly ebbed out into a sea of darkness. For a while, my dad did step in, sensing my loneliness and fragility. He would occasionally take me to breakfast or hunting (which I hated, but I wanted to spend time with him, so I would go). But none of that lasted. After her treatment and return home, everything seemed broken. I think each of us retreated to our own cocoons of security and tried to get through, with all of our brokenness.

Life was never the same.

I began to have nightmares about my mom being hurt and suffering, in which I would try to get to her to help her. I could never quite reach her, always waking, screaming, with sweat streaming down my face and covering my chest and back. These nightmares would continue into adulthood.

We all want to be loved, and we are capable of giving so much love...only sometimes we don't know how, and sometimes we just need to ask for it. Secret keepers and other wounded souls are not always good at asking for love.

I remember when my dad drove me to see my mom in the mental hospital for the first time, and he simply dropped me off and told me where to go. I still don't know why I had to go alone—maybe there was a visitor limitation, or maybe he just didn't want to see her like that. Whatever the reason, I was alone and felt petrified as I approached the inside door. After I stepped off the elevator onto her floor, I felt warm, clammy, with the pain of anxiety and fear growing in the pit of my stomach. What would she be like? What would she look like? Would she remember me? Was she coming home? So many questions swirled through my head.

I stood outside a big, securely-locked, white metal-and-glass door, then heard buzzers and the sound of doors opening and securely shutting. Soon, I saw her approach on the other side, with glazed eyes, in a hospital gown, shuffling forward with tears streaming down her cheeks. After what seemed like an eternity, the door buzzed and I was allowed to walk through to the other side, where they were keeping my mother very secure, like an animal at the zoo.

She must have done something bad to deserve this, I thought.

I looked up at her, she bent down and hugged me, then she asked through teary eyes, "Kevin, do you still love me?"

My body quivered as more warm, salty tears made rivers down my cheeks. "Of course, Mom, of course, I love you!"

That moment remains seared in my memory, and I can see her like it was yesterday. With the guilt and shame eating away at her, and the fear that she was never lovable, and surely was not lovable now. As her little boy, I wanted to rescue her, to take her away and to make everything better. She was my mother, and I did not want anyone to hurt her. My mother, like me, just wanted to be seen, be heard, belong, and be loved.

Her question of "do you still love me?" would become my question of "do you love me?" as I moved through life. The search for unconditional love and acceptance has been a long journey, and I have taken what I learned from that moment with my mom and done some hard work in therapy regarding self-love and acceptance. I am still a work in progress.

And from this question, the next question on my radar would eventually become, "does God love me...really?"

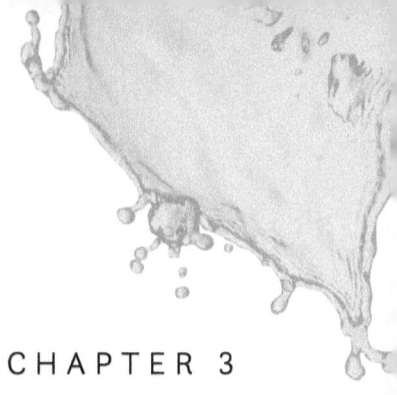

CHAPTER 3

A Seismic Fault in My Faith

FEAR TOOK ROOT EARLY in my life. I think that can happen to all of us—it just depends on whether we are conditioned to embrace the fear, or push through it, with curiosity and confidence. And, sometimes, curiosity can backfire on us and reinforce fear. Such was the case for me, at five years old; yet on the flipside, what happened opened a door for my first positive encounter with faith.

It was a typical evening in our house, as I recall, with my parents sitting at the kitchen table, reading the paper, and talking about their day. I wandered into the kitchen and the pots and pans on the stove caught my attention. Steam, savory smells, and excitement for the upcoming meal overwhelmed my senses. *What was Mom making in the corner pot?*

I could see the steam rapidly rising from the pot and I thought she must be making something yummy for supper. Rather than ask her what was in it, I decided to have a look on my own. Never mind that I was five years old, barely as tall as the stovetop. I reached for it, impulsively, impatiently wanting to know what was inside, thinking if I just tipped it a bit toward me, I could see the delectable contents. Unbeknownst to me, the pot was full to the brim of churning, boiling, steaming water, and as I pulled the pot toward me for a quick look, scalding water trickled down my arm and splashed on my chest. Panic and fear gripped me, and I couldn't think. My reflexes caused me to grip the edge of the pot and pull it, full force, toward me, and the boiling water poured over my chest and body. As I screamed in searing pain, my parents jumped up from the table and ran toward me.

My next memory is waking up in the hospital emergency room.

My mind was starting to settle, the pain easing from medicine, and I looked around the room. I had never been in a hospital.

As I lay in the bed, I noticed the bandages wrapped around my chest and torso. Also, someone was holding my hand. It was a nun who was a nurse. I was at the Catholic hospital. We weren't Catholic, so I had little exposure to nuns, other than the television show with Sally Field, *The Flying Nun*. She was funny and friendly, I thought, so maybe this nun would be, too.

The nurse explained what had happened, what they were doing to help me get better, and that everything would be okay. The majority of the burns were on my chest and torso, as, thankfully, I had not pulled the pot onto my face. She told me the bandages, the dressings, the constant changing of everything, would be painful for a long time, and I would be scarred. And she spoke the truth—I did carry those scars for years, making me very self-conscious about my body.

I was fascinated by this incredibly kind, straightforward woman. Her name was Jenny, and she seemed to have all the time in the world for me. I do not remember anyone else being there, although I am sure my parents were there, too.

The conversations with Jenny kept my mind off the pain. We talked about everything, from animals to sports, and I soon discovered she played softball. I giggled as I imagined a nun, in her habit, hitting the ball and running the bases. She was definitely special, and I could sense she genuinely cared about me. I thought, this is what God must be like—loving, kind, compassionate, accepting, fun, and funny. Otherwise, why else would someone dedicate their whole life to serving Him and wear a habit?!

My time with Jenny was my first positive encounter with faith and kindness, and it was formative. It stuck with me. I will never forget Sister Jenny. I believe she was an incredible manifestation of God in the flesh, and a powerful gift to a scared, injured, and lonely little boy in the hospital. I bet she is hitting homeruns and running the bases somewhere on the other side today!

From this early encounter, I would continue to be drawn to the world of faith. When I was a little boy, often when I was feeling sad, hurt, angry, or afraid, I would stand in my parents' bedroom and stare at an old, framed picture on the wall of Jesus, sitting on a rock in a pasture. He was holding a lamb and surrounded by sheep, looking at them with love and understanding. As I looked at that picture, I could sense the calm, love, and compassion of Jesus. I wanted that, and also wanted to share it. I thought maybe someday I could do something of service, like being a pastor. When people asked me what I wanted to be when I grew up, I would say, "a garbage man or a pastor!" I guess there are similarities—one deals with physical garbage and the other deals with emotional baggage. Since my parents have passed, I have the picture of Jesus, and it will always have special meaning attached to it.

Fear, curiosity, and faith all intersected early in my life, and all had an impact. Little did I know, later in life, I would have a confrontation with faith that would rock my world and derail me for several years. Even the memory of it today still triggers the release of hormones, and my physiological "fight or flight" primal response.

"You should have never been a pastor! It was all a mistake!" The veins in Pastor Larry's neck and face bulged as he shouted those heartbreaking words in my face. I could feel his warm breath and flecks of spittle on my skin. Why was he so angry? Was it jealousy? The breaking of an emotional bond between us? Or a feeling he was being betrayed?

It felt like the air was being sucked out of the room. The lead pastor's office was suddenly small, warm, and stifling. My head was reeling, and I felt the slight knocking of a headache beginning. I was in shock, as I thought how this miserable moment was going to be the final culmination of five plus years of ministry, hard work, and dedication. Don't get me wrong—it was my choice to leave my pastoral role. I knew it was time to resign, as so many things had come to a head—including my own beliefs and theology, emotions, sexuality, and boundaries of friendship and loyalty. I was an empath, desperate for approval and validation, and Larry was a narcissist. He had manipulated me, and used me, to sway public and board opinions in the church while demanding blind-faith loyalty, and our relationship had been unhealthy and codependent. But I hadn't expected it to end with this much venom and vitriol.

I walked out the doors of the church and got into my new (used) red Chevrolet convertible, breathed a sigh of tense relief, put the top down, and drove home as fast as I possibly could. I'd bought the car after I decided to quit. I had been too self-conscious to drive a red convertible as a pastor—wondering what such a choice would say about me. Buying the car felt like an act of rebellion, or a cry for freedom—something I felt as the wind blew through my hair, music pulsing from the radio, cars passing in a blur.

I wondered, *how does God feel about all these decisions?* The freedom I felt in unleashing from the church was mixed with a heaviness, a sense of guilt, shame, uncertainty, and failure. Anxiety quickly crept in, causing my mind to race and my forehead to sweat. I felt an overriding desire to forget and escape, so I drove faster. Little did I then know I was also beginning my swift descent into a darker mental tunnel. A time of flight, hiding, fear, and paranoia.

I knew I was different. Always different.

That's how I felt as a child and teenager. By the time I was seventeen, I began to have attractions to other men, which I brushed off as random, crazy thoughts. Because I could not possibly be thinking that. I dated girls, and I loved spending time with them. And still, I had this longing, this desire, to be close with another man. I denied it and pushed it down. It was not acceptable and on top of that, thoughts of my dad's reaction would make my stomach convulse.

Just when I thought I had put those "impure" thoughts aside (or rather, tamped them down to the depths of my soul), a guy asked me on a date. I was in high school, working in retail, and he shopped at the store where I worked. He was handsome and charming, a ginger with a lean, athletic physique, who was on the swim team at another high school. Never had I expected someone to be so forward—he called the store where I worked and asked me on a date. Shocked and embarrassed, I told him I was not a fag, and I did not want to go out with him. Then I slammed the phone into the cradle, sweating, breathing rapidly, and crying. I ran into the backroom of the store, overwhelmed with emotions, spinning in a circle with cardboard boxes piled all around me. I took a punch at a box, breaking a hole in it. Then I threw my fist into another one, and did it again, and again. Finally, I crumbled to the floor. I stayed there until I could compose myself enough to walk back out and face my coworkers and customers.

In the following days, I was filled with remorse and regret. Remorse for my reaction, my words, and my cruelty. Regret, because I began to ruminate on whether I should have gone out with him.

This was the birth of my sexuality and feelings. I just did not know it at the time.

Believing that was not who or what I really was, I continued to date, until I married my high school sweetheart at nineteen. Surely, these thoughts and feelings would go away, I thought.

They did not, but life went on.

Almost ten years later, after graduating from a religiously affiliated university, I worked in the corporate world, while continuing to feel the tug and desire to serve God and others in a bigger way. Eventually, I went to work for one of the largest churches in the city, with a team of pastors. It was growing rapidly, was conservative yet progressive in ways, and had a rich and deep heritage with the founding pastor. Initially, I hid the fact that I was gay. I was still attracted to other men, an unrelenting yearning deep within that would never abate. At the same time, I was dedicated to living as a married man and father, especially since my duties revolved around other business and creative skillsets. But I finally shared with a small leadership group that I had struggled my entire adult life with being gay.

When I shared this, someone responded, "That's great, and you could be of help to others, if only we had anyone in our congregation like you." I was shocked at their ignorance, as I knew there were many people in the church that were silent sufferers, living in shame and secrecy regarding their sexuality. There was education and awareness that needed to happen on both sides of the fence. On one side, the congregation needed to know that, in a church of 1,200 people, there were approximately five percent potentially wrestling with their sexuality. They needed a safe place to talk about it. Gallup Research reported, in 2022, that the percentage of the population identifying as LGBTQ was 7.1% On the other side, those wrestling with their sexuality needed to know the church loved them, accepted them, and was offering hope and encouragement, versus condemnation. I fought hard to justify my position and point of view, and my passion to help others maintain their religious beliefs alongside their married lives grew into a ministry of the church.

It wasn't long into my tenure at the church before I became acquainted with Exodus International, a nonprofit global umbrella organization connecting ex-gay ministries, that was rapidly growing in strength and numbers. In fact, the soon-to-be president was from my city. I dove in headfirst and developed and led a ministry for those in our city and region wrestling with their faith and sexuality. It's important for me to say that I NEVER said or believed someone could magically change from gay to straight—because I knew it wasn't so for me. Rather, my position was that there must be a way for me (for us) to reconcile our sexuality and the faith that taught us acting on it was wrong; there must be a way for us to maintain our marriages and families. Little did I know, this was really a more public way of working through and processing my beliefs and sexuality, just the very early stages of it.

I really had no idea what I was getting into with Exodus International, nor was I prepared for the people and media frenzy that would follow. A ministry talking theology and talking about being gay and ex-gay (I hated that term), was like throwing meat to the wolves. It created a sensation, with both positive and negative attention, and placed an immense amount of pressure on me, my family, and the church. As with anything controversial, others want to join you, have you adopt their position, and use you to further their agenda. Sometimes, it was challenging for me to discern the sheep from the wolves. At one point, I was selected as pastor of the year for the state. The pressure started to build to also be a voice for political agendas, which was something I never, ever wanted to do.

After one public speaking engagement, my stomach was nauseous, and I knew that I could not maintain the momentum, or the position, others were expecting me to fulfill. Someone in the crowd pointed an angry finger at me and said, "What are you going to do when you find out one of your kids is gay, because one of them will be!" I knew they could be right, it could happen, and then, what would I do? I knew I would love them, but if I wasn't accepting myself, how could I accept them? I walked off the stage, shaking, nauseous, with yet another headache. I knew, in that moment, that I could not do this much longer, and I knew I could not be a political pawn for anyone or anything. I wanted to run far, far away. Instead, I drove home and mowed the lawn.

At the same time, a crisis was brewing within the church.

The church I worked at had been a place where I initially felt safe and secure. It was established by a wonderful family, pillars in the religious community, and along with its respectable heritage, maintained a balanced theology (for a conservative, charismatic Christian church). I described it to others as a "middle of the road" place of worship—solid biblical teachings and doctrine, nice people, worship that was not too ecstatic, with hints of traditionalism. I grew to love the place, and it became the right place to raise our family, even though I knew I could never be openly gay there, only ex-gay, struggling and wrestling with my sexuality, but not living as a gay man. Yet, as time passed and senior leadership positions transitioned, it became apparent many things were going to change. Along with the leadership style, other elements, like worship, began to become more charismatic and emotional. The bedrocks of the church I had once loved, shifted ever so subtly. Eventually, I knew this, combined with my growing discomfort in the public ex-gay role, would necessitate my departure. My mind was exhausted, and I was becoming more agitated and confused by my faith—by organized religion in general. I believed I was probably disappointing God with my decision to leave the ministry; however, I had to take care of myself before I had an emotional meltdown. I realized the time was coming where I would have to figure out how, or if, my gay self fit into all of this, and what I was going to do about it.

I decided to go back into the corporate world—this time, the world of marketing and advertising. (This would become the first place where I felt accepted and welcomed for whomever or whatever I was.) It might have been easier, in some ways, to stay in the pastoral role at the church, but I knew in my gut that resigning and leaving when I did was the best decision for me and, in the long-term, for my family. No matter how hard it became afterward.

After having that volatile meeting with the lead pastor to submit my resignation, I received a veiled message or threat through another associate team member. The message was to keep what had happened, and what had been said, to myself. That it would be in everyone's best interest. I was terrified, as I perceived this as someone threatening to throw my kids out of their private school or come after me in some fashion. Like a papa bear, I would do anything to protect my family, and I also wanted to protect myself, so thus began my period of hiding from the world and from God. I knew I had done the right thing by resigning; however, the question haunted me: Had I done more harm to my family by resigning or would they one day understand that I had done it to protect my integrity and to protect them from beliefs that I could no longer adhere to?

I tried to hide, to outrun it all in my new convertible. But the irony was, if God is omnipotent and omnipresent, He always knows where I am and what I am thinking. Consequently, hiding is impossible. Like the Bible story of Jonah and the whale, where God had a whale swallow him and take him to where he eventually needed to face his truth, situations and circumstances would take me to places where I was forced to face my truth, and determine whether I would allow it to be life-giving or push me to run further, to a place of no return. I learned on my journey the power of the bible verse, "...the truth shall set you free." (John 8:32)

Just like Jonah, not facing my truth, running from my truth, numbing my truth, only created an unbearable bandage. One that felt tighter and heavier over time.

After leaving the church, my job, and a once significant and emotionally dependent relationship with Pastor Larry, I soon realized I needed to talk with a professional counselor. Although I quickly landed in a new marketing profession and found some comfort in the acceptance I felt in that world, I was overwhelmed with feelings of loss, insecurity, displacement, and fear. My children were young and vulnerable, and did not understand why I was leaving the ministry. They loved the church; my office there—with an aquarium, an endless supply of candy, and people who loved to see and talk to them—was a place of fun in their lives. Now, things had shifted dramatically. Church had been a magical place for them; now it became a place I was running from and wanted to avoid, in fear they might be hurt.

I trusted my doctor, confided in him about the stress of the transition, and he referred me to a gentle giant of a therapist. In my first meeting, my palms were clammy with sweat, my heart and mind racing, and even the soles of my feet were perspiring. I grew up believing if you need help, there is something wrong with you! So, instead, I had tried to be tough, figure it out, and suck it up. I was walking into this counselor's office feeling like I had failed on every front. I was disappointed in myself. I fell into the overstuffed, comfy chair opposite my therapist's desk, and wished I could sink deeper and deeper into the cushion, until I ultimately disappeared forever.

At times I thought, *you are just like your mother. Your fate will be the same.* I could relate to her feelings of being trapped, helpless, and afraid.

Losing her at such an early age was an abandonment that is difficult to describe. It was like she died in ways, and I lost the mother I once knew. I think my first experience with this seasoned therapist started the mental process of beginning to acknowledge and feel that early abandonment. Like an onion, it had to be peeled ever so slowly, as there was so much there.

Dr. Ben was disarming, kind, empathetic, and engaging. He made me want to talk. I talked so much that I began to wonder if I would ever run out of things to say to him. His probing questions dove deep into my childhood, my marriage, my sexuality, my faith, and my relationship with the other pastor—and with God.

Looking back, I know he immediately pinpointed two things that were tripping me up. One, my image and relationship with God. Two, my very busy monkey mind, always living in the past or the future, and not in the present. I was particularly confused by the second observation, as I always counted on my motor-mind and ability to think on many levels at once as a gift. I was unique and special, able to think about, feel, and interpret so many things—and people—at once. Later, I would realize I was on the first steppingstone of finding out that special was not quite the word for the myriad of dysfunctional thoughts raging through my brain. Dr. Ben, realizing I thought this attribute was a gift, smiled, and asked me, "Isn't it exhausting to have to think on so many levels all of the time?" He knew something I did not know at the time. It was the beginning of awareness for me, on so many levels. He saw my inability to be in the moment, as well as my people-pleasing attributes that caused me to feel and sense everyone's emotions and feelings—everyone's, that was, except my own—in exchange for validation.

He recommended two books: *God on a Harley,* by Joan Brady, and *The Miracle of Mindfulness,* by Thich Nhat Hanh. I believe he suggested *God on a Harley* to challenge my image of God and the small box I had put my faith in. The book, much like a fairytale, demonstrates what can happen when we drop our egos, be real, and embrace the moment. God shows up, often in unexpected ways, and especially to someone in a traditional mindset like me. I read the book several times, relating to and loving the idea God could show up as a guide, a person with incredible wisdom, patience, and love, and not just discipline and rules.

The Miracle of Mindfulness challenged me to be present in every moment and to start in small ways. (God knew I needed to start very small!) The author suggests being present when you are, for example, washing the dishes, thinking of nothing else but what you're doing, focusing on the dish, the act of washing and drying, etc. I challenged myself to be where my hands are, keep my brain in the room, in the present, and not off thinking about work tomorrow or regretting some action from a few hours ago in the past. I found mindfulness to be much harder than it sounds...and after over ten years of therapy, reading countless books, and listening to meditations and podcasts, I am still working on it. I have made progress, and there is more to make, to learn, and grow, as I still my mind and concentrate on the people, places, and things in my immediate focus. I also began to realize my dad must have struggled with this, too. He always seemed to be somewhere else, looking past me, thinking about something or someone else, enough to where I often had to remind him what we were talking about. My interactions with him eventually began to show me how *I* was interacting with others—appearing distracted, impatient, in a hurry to "get to the point," and not being fully present and connecting with them.

As my conversations with Dr. Ben progressed, he broached the subjects of owning my truth, keeping my sexuality a secret, potential discussions that might be necessary with my wife, as well as my hurt and woundedness regarding the church, my marriage, and my responsibility in all of that. All of this felt daunting, and so, as busyness was my mode of operation, I began to get busier with work, church, and family. Good distractions. This began my period of "isms" to cope, comfort, and numb myself from dealing with the emotional pain, trauma, and truths in my life.

The first was workaholism. After being a "failure and mistake" in the church, I surely was not going to drop the ball in my new career. If I'd learned anything growing up in a midwestern family, it was that hard work solves a multitude of sins. Consequently, I worked hard, climbing the ladder, going after promotions and more money, traveling, and always being available to others. I maintained no boundaries, as boundaries only get in the way. I went in early, stayed late, skipped lunches, attended community events and conferences, worked on vacations, all the while hoping someone would take notice and tell me I was doing a good job. Most importantly, it kept me busy, very busy, with no time to think about or process what was being ignored, moving, and growing deep below the surface. Keep moving, keep hustling, do, do, do, I demanded of myself. And, by all means, do not stop and think about what is happening inside. What I ignored underneath began to manifest instead in my body, and I began to have cluster migraines, fatigue, and pressure in my chest. Similar to my Instant Pot, the pressure was building, only the slow-release valve was not turned on. Eventually, the top would blow off, but not yet.

My second "ism" was familyaholism. I loved my family and still do, more and more. I placed a high bar for myself as a husband and father, and by God, I was going to make it—or exceed it! I vowed to be the best father, make sure my kids knew they were loved, encourage them in all extra-curricular activities, whether sports, dance, gymnastics, or church, and inspire them to dream big (especially as I often beat myself up for not dreaming bigger, and for letting others define me and my abilities). Being a talented codependent and people-pleasing person, I kept the focus on family and work. I have to say, despite my mistakes and dysfunction, I have some of the best and most talented children ever. They are adults now, pursuing big dreams, living domestically and internationally. I would not change anything about the love and encouragement they received from me and their mother. It was a launching pad for them. It also has allowed them to have an expansive world view, to be open, honest, and trans-parent as we have navigated some difficult waters, including my coming out and our divorce, over the past several years. We have accepted, loved, and honored one another amid our differences. We have talked about the mistakes, misconcep-tions, secrets, and the rigidity of our strict faith-based home. I am forever grateful for these three children and to be able to relate to them as genuine, authentic equals on the path of life. All of that said, it is also true that I used my family to distract me. As I placed my laser focus on them, along with work, I was able to avoid looking within.

The third "ism", exercise-ism, rose from my pride in taking care of myself. I was not good at sports, was always the last one picked for a team, and was the chronic choice for bullies in my youth. Consequently, as an adult, I wanted to show myself, and others, that I was strong and capable at something. Ironically, I became a runner. Hmmm...running from myself, my truth, my traumas...it all makes sense now.

Like the other focus areas of my life, I jumped in whole-heartedly. Eventually, I had a dedicated running partner, and I was logging four to five runs, averaging a total of about twenty miles, a week. I became addicted to the rush of endorphins that would surge through my head during and after a run. I felt strong and like I could do anything. I did some races, although no marathons, as I enjoyed running for stress relief, focus, and the relationship I had with my running partner, Zach.

I felt safe with Zach. I eventually came out to him, but he never treated me any differently. I had been so fearful of telling him, and yet, I knew in my heart he would be supportive. When I told him, he focused more on the solution, asking, "Okay, now what are you going to do?" And "what can I do to help you in the process? I will always have your back." He and his wife were always loving and supportive. Zach was an important part of my journey, and we developed a healthy friendship—just two guys on different paths, getting through life. We joked that our runs were like therapy bubbles. We could say and talk about anything, and we both promised to never repeat it. It was a safe and sacred space.

I will never forget when he broke the news to me that they were moving to another state. It was a cool, crisp morning, the sun barely beginning to arc a few rays into the sky. It was 6:20 a.m., when we usually met, and we had just begun our run up the hill. My feet were still feeling like bricks, the coolness of the air was hitting my face, and then he broke the news. I cried, not knowing what he would think about my emotions—but I couldn't help it. I loved Zach. He was like a brother to me. We had been running together for almost fifteen years. I knew I would not get up this early, this many mornings, to torture myself running in the spring, summer, fall, and winter, for anyone else. He was family. He attended all three of my children's high school graduation parties, and my daughter's wedding. He was also one of the first people I told about my sexuality.

My heart broke with the news he was leaving. It meant the relationship would be changing, evolving, become something different. I do not like change in general, and I certainly did not like this one. On top of that, I would miss our runs, too. Between work, family, church, and exercise, I had very little, if any, down time—and I liked it that way. I knew I would not run this much on my own, and I did not know anyone else who could fill his running shoes. These "isms" were my boundaries that keep me on the straight and narrow, or so I thought.

The days rolled on. Zach moved, and I filled the void with exercise classes and other forms of working out. My kids left the nest, one by one, and it was during this time, roughly during the year I met John in Chicago, that my "isms" were not filling the void any longer.

The bubbles were beginning to percolate inside of me, and I began to look for ways to keep the inevitable at bay. I found myself eating more, splurging on decadent chocolates or ice cream, just something to make me feel a little bit better inside. At the same time, I began to shift from what a former coworker called "two-glass chardonnay Kevin" to a three, four, or maybe more-glass guy. My insides were churning, aching; my headaches were mounting; and my anxiety and insecurity were crawling over my body like the tentacles of an octopus grabbing its prey. I wanted it all to stop. I did not want to deal with all the emotions, feelings, unresolved trauma, and resentments trapped deep under the surface.

What was I going to do? I wondered.

My survival techniques were no longer working.

Years before, I had gotten a puppy who had never been kenneled. I had her in the car one day and needed to go through the drive-through at the bank, so I placed her in a little kennel I'd set up on the front seat while I conducted my transaction. Once the kennel door was shut, she realized she was trapped. It didn't matter that I was next to her; she still freaked out. This sweet, adorable, greeting card puppy gnashed her teeth at me. She hissed and snarled like she was in *The Exorcist*, and she began biting the metal door in an insane fit of fury. She was desperate. Once I let her out, she magically transformed back into the sweet, docile little puppy I knew previously.

I could see I was now becoming the crazy puppy—only I was trapped by my own devices and a product of my own making—and I could not imagine or see a way out of the elaborately picture-perfect life and world I had created over many years. My coping devices and life itself were the metal bars across the front of my cage, and I could not see how to open the door.

Opening the door would involve truth, honesty, integrity, bravery, authenticity, determination, grit, and hard work. It was a far bigger undertaking than anything I had ever imagined or thought that I desired. I wanted to stay in my cage, I did not really want to be free.

I wanted to get through life, make the other people in my life happy, and somehow find a way to be semi-happy—nothing big, just semi-happy. I could not bear the thought of letting others down, hurting them, and worst of all, I was beginning to believe that I did not know who I really was or what I wanted. And then there was the bigger question: Did it really matter anyway?

The darkness inside me had grown since realizing the logistics of my relationship with John would never work. He was too far away; and, also, I was not feeling emotionally prepared or ready to fully come out to everyone. The grief over thinking I had missed out on a soulmate was too much to carry, in addition to my fears and my crumbling marital relationship.

The pressure cooker was now on high, and the quick release valve was still not open. I was slipping into hopelessness and despair. Knowing I could not any longer live with one foot in and one foot out, I began to think of an escape route. Running away was not an option. Coming out as gay after coming out once as ex-gay, was not an option. Everyone, most importantly, God, would be disappointed—and where would I spend eternity? My mind, heart, and body continued sinking into what felt like a tar pit. Hot bubbling thoughts of worthlessness, hopelessness, failure, and potential loss scalded and enveloped me. I began thinking, *I haven't gone too far down the path. There is still time to end this dark game. Yes, I have an option. One that will set me free, and one where everyone else will ultimately be happier.*

Yes, acceptance, fear, and sadness came to rest in the gut of my stomach. It was time to be brave, or, what I then considered brave. Time to break free from the cage, liberating myself and those around me. *I am sorry, God. I really am.*

CHAPTER 4

The Endless Tunnel

I WALKED THROUGH THE door of the restaurant, which was loud with the clamoring of dishes and clinking of glassware. The scent of sizzling burgers and chicken wafted through the air.

I wasn't hungry, but Garret had asked me to have lunch. He was my best friend, so I came, even though the day felt dreary, stormy, like I had a damp, dark towel over my head, obstructing my view and my thoughts.

I grabbed a high-top table, content to sit alone with my thoughts for a few minutes, as he normally ran late.

Garret and I had known each other for several years. He worked for one of my clients, and since we both had a coffee addiction, we often found ourselves in the basement break room while waiting for a pot to brew. One day, we struck up a conversation and there was instant chemistry. I felt I had known him all my life. We often joked that we were brothers from another mother—and it would have to be another mother, because he was a fair-skinned ginger, and I was much darker in coloring.

Since I was little, I had yearned for a brother. Someone to teach me how to be a guy, to confide in, to be playful with, to look out for me. Someone who would see me, so I could be real. The universe fulfilled that request, albeit much later, when Garret entered my life, and we became fast friends. Both of us were in great shape and loved doing hot yoga and working out, along with going to shows, and yes, drinking lots of coffee together, while laughing and talking about life. I was grateful for him; however, even now, it seemed like it was not enough. I was showing up because it was Garret, but otherwise I would have canceled. I was in a dark place.

I caught a glimpse of sunlight as he came through the door and headed to the table. We hugged and then began our ritual of catch-ups on the day, work, family, and more. We ordered lunch, and we were not far into the conversation when he asked how I was doing. Being a people pleaser, I have always struggled verbalizing the reality of my thoughts and feelings about myself. This time, though, was different, as I picked at my grilled chicken salad and rearranged lettuce leaves in my bowl, my eyes downcast. There wasn't much else to say besides the truth.

Unable to look him in the eyes, I told him I was not in a very good place, mentally. I shared how dark everything felt, and that I saw no answers and no hope for my current situation regarding my sexuality and my marriage. "I don't know if I can keep going," I said.

Garret quickly picked up on the cues. He didn't shame me or offer easy platitudes, like things weren't that bad, or it would get better. Rather, he told me about a counseling group his brother attended that had really changed his thinking and helped him process his feelings and emotions. He suggested that maybe I should try it.

I was ambivalent, and didn't have the motivation or desire to do something like that. It was too late for me, I thought—too dark, too hopeless. He gently persisted, though, and asked if his brother could call me and tell me about the group. Slightly annoyed, I agreed and, after paying the bill, I headed to my car.

I was thankful for Garret. I knew he genuinely loved and cared for me like a brother, but that was not enough to keep me going at this point. I felt all the energy and life had been sucked from my mind and body. Tiredness, fatigue, sadness, and a sense of purposelessness engulfed me once again.

Darkness swirled around me, and I couldn't clear my head. All I could think about was that I did not want to go back to work. Then my cell phone rang, jolting me from my toxic thinking. It was David, Garret's brother. *Good grief*, I thought. Garret must have called him from the parking lot and told him how bad I was!

David was also a loving, compassionate, and forward individual. He firmly suggested I visit his group the following night. He would talk with the counselor in advance, he told me, and I would go as his guest. There was no need to argue, fuss, or fight—he made it clear he was taking me. My pessimism raged, but I relented; and a tinge of relief even shimmered across my brain. *I can put off my plans for another day or maybe a few days*, I thought. The goodbye letters I'd written to my wife and kids would keep. Knowing someone cared about me and was throwing me a reason to wait on any actions, without offering clichés or promises, but simply recognizing my desperation and fragile state—offering to walk alongside me without judgement and hold my hand for a bit—made a difference. *One more day. I will try to make it one more day.*

That decision to try to make it one more day wasn't an easy one.

I had lost all hope. I hardly knew any longer what the word even meant; it had always been associated with God and my faith, and how could I feel hope in God, if I believed he rejected me and did not love me? Apathy and paralysis encompassed me, and I didn't feel like I could ever attain anything I deeply wanted. And I certainly didn't think the complicated events of my life would improve or lead to something better.

The crazy thing is I am generally an optimist to the core, often chided for being too upbeat and positive. But my tank was on empty.

At some point, while everything was converging on me, I made the decision that leaving this life would be the best decision for myself and everyone around me.

How noble, right? Now, I don't see it that way, but I have also found grace for myself as I was in that moment. It can be hard for people who haven't wrestled with suicide ideation, and the depth of depression and dark night of the soul that goes along with it, to understand why someone contemplates this as a solution. But in this state of mind, it can feel like the only way out.

For me, the thought started as a fleeting whisper in my ear. Then it took root in my brain, where it continued to take space, grow, and develop into a full-blown plan. One night, home alone, still grappling with my inability to reconcile my marriage, sexuality, and faith, I tearfully removed several sheets of paper from the computer printer. I sat down at the kitchen island, poured a big glass of white wine, and began to write goodbye letters to each member of my family. The regret, grief, sorrow, and shame all came crashing down on me. It felt like sadness and desperation were burying me alive, and I couldn't get out from underneath any of it. This was my reality, and so this was my plan. I carefully sealed each envelope, my hands shaking, and salty tears landing on the flap of each one.

Then my cell phone went off, startling me and bringing me back to reality.

It was John, whom I hadn't heard from for a long time. We had maintained our long-distance friendship, although he had been giving me an extended period of space and time, as he knew I was struggling with our relationship. He also never called in the evenings. Yet, in that moment, I had come to his mind, and he decided to pick up his phone to see how I was doing. We talked, and after I hung up, I was able to take a deep breath. I went to sit outside on the deck, feel the breeze on my face, and listen to the birds singing in the redbud tree. I was able to make it through another day.

Reflecting back on that night, I know it was a God thing. One of the many miracles that would happen in my life—like David insisting I attend his group—to redirect, refocus, and cause me to pause amid my plans.

I felt the hand of God again not too many nights later, tossing and turning in a fitful sleep, my mind and soul feeling the weight of my burdens.

Peaceful rest eluded me.

It was warm, and I was lying on top of the covers, as the air conditioner didn't circulate well on the upper level of our house. The ceiling fan was spinning and clicking, and I was in the state between awake and asleep when I suddenly felt a presence in the room.

I rolled over to my right and looked towards the dresser across from me, against the wall. In the corner next to it, I could see a figure. It seemed a little grainy, bluish-gray, almost like a hologram. As the fog settled in my mind, my vision sharpened on the apparition. What, who, how? The realization was gradually settling in—it was my grandfather. My grandpa from the farm. My grandpa who'd loved me, held my hand, spent time with me. The man who'd meant more to me than anyone would ever know. He was standing in the room looking at me with love and compassion in his eyes.

I am not sure if he spoke or if I heard his thoughts. He said, "Kevin, it is not time for you. Don't do it. I love you." And in an instant, he was gone.

I dropped my head back into bed thinking I surely must have lost my mind. It took me hours to fall back to sleep.

Something about what and how he said it resonated with me, and I knew it was true. I knew it was him. I always felt he was with me after his passing, like a guardian angel. I have his picture sitting on my desk as I write this book, and he is still watching over me.

I guess desperate times call for desperate measures, and he revealed himself to me.

It was a sobering experience and, most importantly, it stopped me from moving forward with my plan.

I believed my grandpa, as I knew he loved me, and if he said it was not time, well then, no matter how bad I wanted to be with him, it was not time.

I destroyed the goodbye letters I had written to my family. Yet, getting through each day was still a struggle.

Looking back, how did I get here? How did the darkness get so thick and suffocating I was considering ending my life? Hopelessness had taken a chokehold in my sexuality, marriage, and my faith. My black and white thinking left me with only one solution: eliminate me, the problem would be solved, everyone would be happier, and I would be at peace. I did not realize how twisted and distorted my thinking had become. Looking at the complexities of each of these areas now helps me understand the path that led me to contemplate my self-destruction.

What began as a beautiful awakening back in Chicago evolved into something more complex, where more than one thing was true. I began to realize the depth of my sexuality and the pressing need to deal with it, for my sanity, and for those in my life. Infidelity and secret-keeping became parts of my journey. John was an incredible soul, who taught me things about myself I needed to face and know. Unfortunately, infidelity makes an already difficult situation worse. It further erodes trust, and I began living with deception and lies, covering my tracks like an animal, along the way. While this may work in the short-term, it was not the way for me to resolve conflict or build healthy relationships. Gay or straight, infidelity was my choice, and it was a slippery slope that led to more isolation and hiding, and reinforced my childhood role as a secret keeper. Now, I was not only hiding my inner truth, but also the truth around my actions. In addition, I had broken a sacred vow I made to my wife and to God. I tried to rationalize my decision by using my sexual orientation as the scapegoat; however, I know I could have left my marriage prior to beginning a relationship, so I could not blame having an affair on being gay.

A few counselors advised me to leave and divorce, with no admission of what had happened. They felt it was unnecessary and would cause more harm and hurt than anything else—just leaving was a "clean" way out. There was no need to share the truth. But I knew I could not do that, as I loved and respected my wife. Even if it might be easier on her, she deserved more, and I needed to start being honest and truthful, with her and with myself. Yet, the thought of this made me feel like I was carrying a load of bricks on my shoulders, with a gnawing pit growing in my stomach. This had made me physically and emotionally sick and drove me deeper into my cave of secrets, where I did not want to see anyone or anything, beyond embracing that I was a total failure. I just wanted a way out. And I'd decided maybe there was a way out, where no one would have to know my secret(s), not even her, and I could leave everyone better off—financially, and with their memory of who and what they thought I was, with their world left intact.

My guilt and despair were intertwined around my marriage, and my sexuality was also weighing on me. I could never see myself living fully out as a gay man. The mask I had worn for years was too tight, well-fitted, painful, and yet comfortable. It was all I had ever known. The media was full of stereotypes of gay men and their escapades. I certainly did not see myself like that—flamboyant and effeminate. Also, where were the healthy gay people or relationships? I didn't see them portrayed on screen, and I didn't know anyone gay and truly accepting of it and happy in real life.

I realize now I had spent my life afraid others would "see the real me" and think I was gay, so when I saw something that made me think of being gay, it made me recoil and cringe—like touching the hot stove. In reality, I did see myself, in some way, in the characters portrayed in the media and I saw myself, too, in the lives of many unhappy people I knew. In my life, I had always looked outside myself for answers. I would spend my time asking myself, what does he or she think? What would they do? What are their feelings and emotions? I was unhappy, and I didn't know how to look within to find my own answers and my own contentment. Self-acceptance is a powerful art, and I was not there, in any way, shape or form. Self-love goes hand in hand with self-acceptance, and I could not offer myself that either. I did not know how.

At times during this period (and even beyond it), I felt like a skittish feral cat at someone's backdoor, pacing, peering in the window of another life. I desired something different but at the same time, was afraid of what would happen if I actually got it. Let me in, feed me, touch me; no, wait—don't do that, the risk is too great.

Anxiety, tension, and racing thoughts of the endless risks associated with changing my life plagued me. The imagined losses seemed insurmountable. I might lose my job, my relationships, my family, my parents, my church, the respect of others—the list went on and on.

At times, I felt like I was suffocating, gasping for air with a pillow firmly planted over my face. I began having panic attacks. My chest would tighten, my breathing quickened, beads of sweat formed on my forehead—I felt trapped, caged, and oh my God, I needed to get out! Being the ultimate people pleaser and chameleon, I thought I would need to sacrifice myself in order to save myself and others from my brutal truth. For a long time, I believed the most possible for me, one day, was to live a celibate life, alone, as a privately gay man. I thought I would never ever live as an openly gay man—and never live openly in a relationship with another man. It was all pain; layers and layers of compressing pain.

As part of it, I was still trying to reconcile my faith with having left the church and ministry years before. My role had gone significantly beyond my work with our congregation. During my tenure as a pastor in the 90s, I was an ex-gay poster child. At least that's what it felt like by the end of my time in the ministry and with Exodus International.

Initially, it had seemed like a perfect world. I could have my faith and eat it, too (oops—I meant cake!) I could be out, sort of, as previously gay, accepted by the church as long as I was committed to not living my sexuality out.

My faith was a huge component of my life, and I desperately wanted to reconcile my faith with my sexuality. It was like pushing a big boulder up a hill. It was barely possible, even if it rolled over me a few times. My time with Exodus International, for a time, felt like one way to push that boulder up higher.

Exodus International was founded in 1976 as a global, interdenominational, ex-gay umbrella organization that recruited and connected other groups and organizations that sought to support the movement. It had over four hundred local ministries, across seventeen countries, and many denominations. Member groups varied in their beliefs, with some promoting reparative therapy practices and others offering support groups for those trying to live in a marriage and/or a Christian faith environment while limiting their homosexual desires. The ministry I led fell into the latter. I always knew I was gay; it didn't change. I wanted to create a supportive place for others, like me, who wanted to live in accordance with their faith beliefs and marriage vows.

The need for support was great, and people drove from surrounding communities and towns across the state to attend our meetings and conferences. It was a happy place for me, for a while. What I didn't anticipate, nor did I ever want, was the media frenzy it created. As word spread—both positive, negative, and controversial—the onslaught of media requests and coverage bombarded me. I, sometimes reluctantly, did my best to represent the church and its doctrine, comingled with my personal beliefs.

This became increasingly challenging for me. As the dynamics in the church power and politics shifted, I felt increased pressure to hold a certain point of view that wasn't aligned with my own beliefs. This was my perception and interpretation. Regardless of whether it was an accurate reflection of the church leadership's intentions, my internal struggle with the church landscape and my gay feelings started to feel unbearable. Like the *Star Wars* scene when Luke, Leia, Han, and Chewie are trapped in the trash compactor room—all the walls were closing in on me. I had doubt, questions, and fears in my mind about God; the church; being gay; the power, drive to control, and nature of man; potential banishment from the church community. I could go on and on. Everything was closing in on me and I had to get out, so I did.

In an interesting parallel, in 2013, the then president and executive director of Exodus International, Alan Chambers, shut down the global organization. After being at the helm for thirteen years, he and other leaders acknowledged the harm that had been done by the movement. Reparative therapy had, unquestionably, caused damage, contributing to mental health challenges and many suicides and suicide attempts internationally.

Chambers's story is detailed in his memoir *My Exodus: From Fear to Grace,* and the downfall of the organization is chronicled in the documentary *Pray Away.* Another more disturbing film that centers on the controversies surrounding this organization was *Boy Erased,* with Nicole Kidman and Russell Crowe. The movie chronicles the journey of a young gay man, his Baptist pastor father, and his mother, as they have their son undergo a more radical reparative therapy and live-in ministry.

Exodus International was on the forefront of controversy, culture, and religion. I felt guilty both for leaving it behind, and guilty for being a part of it.

I came to the point where I knew I had to leave, but that alone didn't give me peace. Far from it.

I didn't love or accept myself. I didn't believe God did either.

I was trying to live up to my image of God's standard. Trying to perform at my best, say and do all the right things. I was a rule follower at heart, and I knew I couldn't do it. People in the church used to joke about the doctrine, "Don't drink, dance, or chew, or go with girls or guys who do." I could avoid those things, but what about being gay? In my mind, it was the unforgiveable sin, and I couldn't get away from it. And now I had left the ministry, too—who leaves a calling like that? I knew I had left a large number of people in the groups I'd led without a leader. I felt like a total failure on every front, defeated and deflated.

At this point in my journey, therapy had helped in many areas, but my rigid thinking about God and my sexuality was a roadblock to continued progress. Living inside my darkened mind felt like times I'd spent driving down an endless tollway, with road construction narrowing traffic down to one, backed-up lane, trapped with no upcoming exits or turns, just one miserable lane all the way to the final destination. I was driving down that one-lane road, smelling leaking gasoline, the burn in my nostrils warning me that maybe I was headed in the wrong direction, that something was not quite right. And all I could think about was that I was going to hell. Maybe I could pre-empt that by taking things in my own hands, with a sudden turn, and roll off the road.

We are each unique in our circumstances and traumatic events that combine to impact our lives; however, we often end up in similar places, dealing with similar issues like fear, shame, insecurity, abandonment, confidence, sexuality, and our faith. I had arrived in a deadly storm that blended a number of factors from my childhood and my current life, to result in an extreme crisis situation. Fortunately, at its deadliest moment, people were showing up for me, as if responding to an energetic call.

I was only beginning to see it.

Garret and David, gentle in their spirits, wise in their experience, and firm in their approach, threw me a life preserver as I was drowning. I was reluctant, but I also did make the decision to attend the group with David.

At that moment, that was all I knew. I could not think any further than that.

CHAPTER 5

Choosing to Live

"When you lose hope, you fall into apathy—
and then you do nothing."

—Jane Goodall

WHEN I WENT WITH David to his counseling group for the first time, I was nervous and tense. I generally found it easier to talk with people one-on-one versus in a group setting, and what was going on in my life felt even harder to share. But I knew David would be at my side. Even though we did not know each other well yet, I could sense his empathy and a deep understanding and love that flowed from his own life's experiences. This helped to counterbalance the anxiety I felt.

The group was something I was not familiar with previously, a Dialectical Behavioral Therapy (DBT) skills group based on the original program and materials of Dr. Marsha M. Linehan, where skills are taught in a group setting regarding mindfulness, interpersonal effectiveness, emotion regulation, distress tolerance, and conflict management. The local counselor leading the group found it effective in treating a wide range of psychological and emotional issues.

The meeting was held in a small room in an older red brick office building, and when David and I walked in the room together, I saw about fifteen folding chairs that wrapped around in a circle. It was a tight fit. Two tiny windows on the top of the wall made it feel like we were having a secret meeting in someone's basement.

As we entered the circle, Janet, the counselor, looked up and greeted me. My eyes met hers, and in that instant something happened. I felt a sense of peace, of belonging, of acceptance. *How could that be?* I thought. I didn't know her or anyone else here, besides David. Crazy! As I settled into my seat, I looked at her again and felt such an aura of contentment. She had a beautiful smile and reminded me of someone with southern charm and hospitality, like Oprah Winfrey. Even though my palms were damp, and I could feel the tension in my shoulders and upper back, I knew this was going to be a safe place for me.

She opened the group with introductions and then shared a quote for us to contemplate and talk about. Then she began the teaching time, which was followed by applications—either a discussion or role play, or both. There was also a co-facilitator, and they usually played good cop, bad cop, which always made for a lively discussion. It was a very interactive process, and while I immediately felt at ease with Janet, the process itself made me a little uneasy. Yet, I persevered through the first meeting. And kept coming. It felt like the place that I needed to be.

It would take me a few months to come out to this group. When I finally did, it was the first place and group of people I told. On the day I was planning to share this, I was sweating, my throat tightened from nerves. And yet, once I revealed this piece of myself, everyone was accepting.

I learned so much during this period of my life. The group, coupled with my continuing individual therapy, taught me how to effectively process my emotions and not be driven by them. I learned to own my truth, even if I was still a work in progress regarding living it out. I also had to face my rigid thinking and my judgments, and stretch and develop my mind to consider the dialectical in all things.

I had been raised to see things from one perspective, but the group taught me that more than one thing can be true. The world is made of opposites and opposing views, and I came to see that holding a rigid perspective in such a world can increase mental health issues. Through my time with the group, I learned to look for the kernel of truth in various perspectives. I would ask, what is based on fact and what is based on emotion? This helped me to accept others, accept their point of view, and appreciate what they brought to the table, even if I did not necessarily agree with them.

While being a part of this group, I also experienced and learned the reality of love in action from this quote from the famous children's book *The Velveteen Rabbit,* by Margery Williams. "'Real isn't how you are made,' said the Skin Horse. 'It's a thing that happens to you. When a child loves you for a long, long time, not just to play with, but REALLY loves you, then you become Real.'"

I felt loved, really loved, by the others in the group, who became dear friends that remain in my life today, even after many years. It was an incredible experience of personal growth, development, and acceptance that both changed and saved my life. Thank you, David, for helping me on my path to becoming real.

This period of time changed the course of my life. It was characterized by deep inner growth, arising from therapy and our DBT group, as well as other teachers and avenues of healing and restoration that crossed my path. I will touch on my experience with four of the transformational experiences that made a profound difference in my recovery, growth, and healing: journaling, Body Memory Recall (BMR), Regenerating Images in Memory (RIM), and Eye Movement Desensitization and Reprocessing (EMDR).

As much as I love to write, the discipline of journaling was initially tough for me. My mind and body were always moving so fast. It was difficult for me to slow down my thoughts and feelings long enough to capture them on paper. It was recommended, though, by my first counselor, and so I continued, nonetheless. I began by taking my notebook to therapy sessions and writing down important insights and actions steps. Later, I would reflect on my sessions with a journal entry. I also used it to record significant dreams, to express gratitude, and to process through difficult and challenging situations. Sometimes I would write letters to people, expressing my thoughts, feelings, and emotions. These were pure therapy for me, as writing often diffuses the emotions and supports my processing, helping me land in a more balanced place of serenity. The letters also became my tool for thinking through the pros and cons of a potential confrontation, discussion, reconciliation, or decision.

I felt journaling's powerful effect in my own life, and eventually learned there was research that reflects my positive experience. According to the University of Rochester Medical Center, journaling can help individuals manage anxiety, reduce stress, and cope with depression. It can also help control symptoms and improve mood.

It's a safe place to let everything spill out and helps me stay in a healthy mental state. Especially as I have a good friend who also acts as a "journal burning buddy," in the event something unexpected happens and the journals are left behind. Journals are meant to be candid, raw, unfiltered, and for your eyes only. Thus, the book burning! (Although my journals might make for a crazy bestseller one day.)

Another modality that was a deep gift to me at this time was Body Memory Recall (BMR). In the past, I had never been drawn to things like massage therapy, as I had a phobia about someone touching my body.

As my anxiety, tension, and stress had continued to grow over time, I'd noticed the buildup in my body. I constantly felt tightness and knots in the muscles of my neck and upper back area. After a couple of years of doing hot yoga and some regular yoga, I was just starting to get the message that I should listen to my body. At this time, I also became aware of a strange phenomenon in my chest and heart area. There is a backward bend pose in yoga called Camel Pose, that asks you to kneel on the floor, hands on your lower back, and begin to lean backward, lifting and opening your heart and chest. I could not do it. More than that, I felt like I was going to vomit every time I tried. I was frustrated, and I wondered, what are my body and heart trying to tell me?

When I saw some information regarding Body Memory Recall, and its founder, Jonathan Tripodi, on the website of a local healing arts organization, I followed the breadcrumbs and started to explore. The premise of BMR is that our bodies store everything that happens to us in life—the trauma, stress, tension, and memories. BMR is a gentle form of hands-on therapy that supports the body in releasing these toxic components. After learning more and reading Tripodi's book *Freedom From Body Memory*, I decided to find a licensed BMR therapist and reluctantly try.

As I walked into the downtown studio, I noticed the high ceilings, exposed brick, multistory windows, and the smell of incense wafting through the air. I headed down a staircase to a reception area and my BMR therapist, Angie. On that first visit, Angie concentrated on my neck and head for an hour. I lost myself in time, sinking deep within as my body released tensions and anxieties built up over years. When she was done, I thought I had only been there for fifteen minutes. Overwhelmed with peace and tranquility, I knew I would return.

I did. Many times.

Angie eventually worked on my whole body, sometimes bringing me to tears with the healing and releasing power of this bodywork. Eventually, I was able to do Camel Pose, fully extending and opening my chest and heart. I sobbed, feeling truly open for the first time in my life. It was a beautiful and spiritual day for me, and one that I will never forget.

Angie was a teacher I'm thankful showed up on my path, and BMR was another important step in my journey toward healing and living my truth.

Following my BMR journey, a friend told me about Dr. Deb Sandella, the founder of the RIM Institute, and author of the international bestseller *Goodbye, Hurt & Pain, 7 Simple Steps to Health, Love and Success*. RIM® (Regenerating Images in Memory) is a body-centered, transformational technique that helps free you of negative thoughts, feelings, and memories, so you are empowered to live your best life. And it made a profound difference for me.

After I heard about RIM, I read Deb's book, and eventually did a discovery call with her. I was so impressed by her, the methodology, and its foundation in neuroscience, as well as her track record. I did a session with her, followed by a few more sessions over the following months with one of her facilitators.

Hour long sessions seemed like minutes.

The method is hard for me to describe. I can't adequately explain how it works. But it truly did release me from long-held emotional pain.

In one session, as I regressed into some memories, some I was not even consciously aware of previously, I heard my mother say to me, "I release you." I had carried a lifetime of guilt for not being able to save her from her mental illness and other suffering, to the point where I would even have recurring dreams, hearing her call my name and yell for help. As I tried to get to her, my leg would break and I would be pulling, scraping myself across the ground, desperately reaching for her...and I never made it. And through my RIM sessions, there was real release. Release from any expectations she may have had of me, release from the unhealthy codependency, and release from the guilt and shame I had carried all these years, related to my inability to help her.

I am so grateful for Dr. Sandella and her facilitator, who both showed up for me and helped me discover new depths in my healing journey.

Another modality I explored with some of my individual psychotherapy sessions was Eye Movement Desensitization and Reprocessing (EMDR) in a couple of forms.

EMDR uses either a pendulum light on a computer or a

lightbox to send signals through the eyes to the brain, which can lessen the impact of the emotional distress normally felt with thinking about or being triggered by a past traumatic event. The process involves revisiting past memories, and in one of my sessions, we went way back, to a memory of the little eleven-year-old boy I once was, sitting on my bed. I was wearing khaki pants and a brown argyle sweater vest over a tan short-sleeved shirt. When I first recalled this memory, feelings of fear and abandonment—the emotions I had felt in the past during this moment—washed over me, gripping me, paralyzing me. But as we processed the memory using EMDR, I could, over time, feel the tense grip of these emotions melting from my head down, like snow on a mountain on a sunny day. Eventually, I could see the little boy I was, and see myself as the adult I had become holding him, telling him, "It's okay. You are safe. You are loved. You are valuable. You are not alone." This particular image and the process have stuck with me, creating a greater sense of calm, when I find myself beginning to landslide back into my traumatic feelings.

Another effective form of therapy on my path to healing and understanding how my past impacted my present, was simply noticing how I was seeing things. I realized that, up until that point, I had still been seeing my life, my circumstances, and the world through the eyes of a little boy. I next realized it was time to begin seeing it through the eyes of a man. A man living authentically and growing in his truth.

Sometimes I feel like my journey has been a long one, and it is not over yet. However, I must remind myself that I am a work in progress, and as long as I am open and willing, there will be people, places, and things on my path to help me keep moving forward.

The other side of this coin is that not everyone will help us on our journey or be able to walk with us through it. There are detractors in our lives, naysayers, people who live in negativity, act without empathy, or are completely oblivious to the struggles others face. And there are simply those who aren't yet as self-aware, or perhaps, like the Velveteen Rabbit, more "real." Once you start to become more self-aware and real yourself, it can feel more difficult to spend time and interact with those in our lives who haven't yet crossed this bridge.

This makes me think of some conversations I had with a family member in the last few years, before their passing. We talked about a variety of things together, but anything personal, emotional, or raw, was not in our repertoire. One day, though, with a pain in the pit of my stomach and apprehension in my voice, I opened up more deeply, and told them I had struggled with suicide ideation in my darkest times. They could not comprehend it, and told me they couldn't understand that thinking, that I had so much to live for, and such thoughts were selfish.

This response isn't helpful for people who have struggled with such pain.

What individuals often need is just to know someone genuinely cares about them. No reasoning, arguing, shaming, or discounting their thoughts will do what a few words or actions of caring can do to save a life.

A great example of this can be seen at Japan's Tojinbo Cliffs, known as the Suicide Cliffs. At the time of this writing, the suicide rate in Japan is the highest in the developed world; countless people make the trek to these legendary cliffs to bring an end to their lives. A seventy-three-year-old retired policeman, named Yukio Shigi, was determined to make a difference, and so for fifteen years he has watched the cliffs and talked 609 people down from jumping to their deaths. When asked how he did it, he said, "The way I save people, it's like I'm seeing a friend. It's not exciting or anything. I'm like, 'Hey, how are you doing?' These people are asking for help. They're just waiting for someone to speak with them."[1]

We all want someone to care, to speak to us, especially in our darkest hour.

Garret and David were my cliff watchers. They enabled me to go on, seek health and healing. It wasn't as simple as going to one meeting or even going to months of meetings. But it was the seed that helped me begin to prepare for a life I had not even imagined. A life that would begin by being on my own, all alone, for the first time in over fifty years.

---

1 Jonathan Kaiman, "At Japan's Suicide Cliffs, He's Walked More than 600 People Back from the Edge," *LA Times*, February 2, 2018, https://www .latimes.com/world/asia/la-fg-japan-suicide-20180222-story.html.

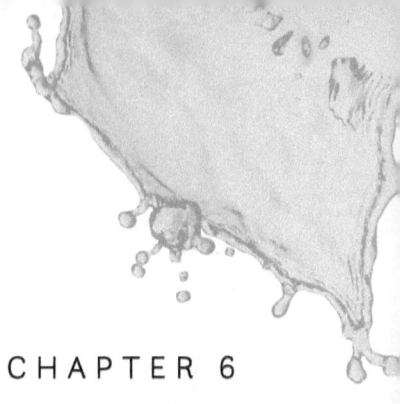

CHAPTER 6

Reconstruction Takes Time

"YOU WILL NEVER BE able to live in a healthy relationship with someone else until you learn how to live alone."

These words were spoken by my therapist on numerous occasions. It was a loaded sentence, as I knew it was no easy task. Learning to live alone—learning to be okay alone—meant overcoming my insecurities, learning how to love and value myself, and facing my demons and fears. All overwhelming ideas I had run from for a long time. I had never lived alone my entire adult life. After living with my parents for the first nineteen years of my life, I then married and lived with my wife for over thirty years. The thought of being on my own scared the hell out of me, and I really did not know if I could do it. Would I fail at this too? Like I perceived I had failed in my marriage, sexuality, and ministry?

I had spent much of the past year separated from my wife. After spending some months in my counseling group and exploring other healing modalities, I eventually came to a point where I knew I had to address my marriage with my wife, and, after having some difficult conversations, I had moved in with a close friend, Lance.

What a rough year it had been!

I missed my wife, the house, the dogs, the seeming normalcy of life.

Lance was a kind man who allowed me to rent a bedroom in his house while I tried to figure things out. I had been there seven months before the holidays hit, when my emotions surged with sentimental memories and lots of tears. Just prior to Christmas, I moved back home, in one final valiant effort to try and make things work.

Life was still feeling incredibly difficult. I was not doing well, emotionally, mentally, or spiritually, and then my mother died suddenly. Dealing with major grief, on top of my sexuality and a failing marriage, was overwhelming.

My DBT group and other therapies helped me make it through, eventually teaching me the truth of Brené Brown's insight that "When we choose growth over perfection, we immediately increase our shame resilience." I could not see it at the time, but I was walking on a pathway of healing and restoration. This healing was at times challenging, brutal, emotional, and even heart-breaking. It was also the slow, cumulative result of continuing to put one foot in front of the other as I walked this winding path. However, there were breakthroughs, ah-ha moments, and times when others pointed out and recognized the growth before I did.

Unfortunately, my home environment was not necessarily as supportive of this growth. My wife was also wrestling with our crumbling marriage, new realities, and a changing life. My friends and chosen family helped keep me accountable and focused on healing and growth throughout this additional layer of challenge, and I also began to see and understand more deeply my wife's perspective and fears. Still, it was a tense environment, pounding with escalating anxiety. It felt like when you're preparing for a storm, putting food rations and water in the basement, boarding up the windows, and piling up sandbags, knowing the crash will hit with full force at some point and time. We both had to establish boundaries to keep ourselves emotionally and psychologically safe. After a while, it simply became too much. The storm was here.

I knew what I needed to do.

I needed time and space (alongside continued therapy) to process my losses, take a breath, just be, and make a plan for self-care for the future. If I did not do this, I would end up back in the depths of the dark, downward spiral of depression and thinking of self-harm. The outcome would not be good for myself or anyone else in my life.

I needed to move out of my family home once more.

One day, over lunch, I began to search online for available apartments, and sensed an inkling of excitement, anticipation, and also fear. My mind buzzed with a counterattack and rationalized all kinds of reasons to not do this now, or to not trek out alone. Maybe I should look for a roommate, I thought, or rent a room again, or part of someone's home? But I told myself—no. It was time to grow up, face my fear, and look for my own place, no matter how small it might have to be. (Little did I know, how small it actually would be!)

I made some appointments to view what I deemed "affordable" units and began my search. The first basement unit I saw was dark, musty, and damp, with old appliances and no washer and dryer. It was downright depressing. After that visit, I decided I did not need to be moving anywhere, anytime soon, on my own. But after a few more weeks, I reignited my search.

I decided I could live without a garage and a bedroom, which opened up the possibility of studios in nicer communities. A dear friend of mine, Mary, had lived in a peaceful, beautiful community on a small lake at the edge of town, following the breakup of her long-term relationship. She had talked of walks around the lake, the ducks and geese, kind neighbors, and the healing, Zen feeling she felt in the environment. It sounded like the place for me, as I could use some peace and healing in my life, so I decided to check the community out for myself.

Pulling up the curved drive into the parking lot, I was struck by its beauty. Non-motorized boats, kayaks, and people fishing dotted the lake and its perimeter. As I stepped out of my car, the air smelled fresh, clean, with the scent of possible rain. Even the overcast sky didn't dampen my optimistic outlook on my potential new home.

Walking into the office, I was greeted by the leasing agent, Katherine. She only had one studio available, so off we went on a tour of the community and the unit. When she opened the door, I saw it was a galley-type layout, very tight and tiny, with barely room for a bed. The only space to eat was at a small kitchen island with room for a stool or two. But on the plus side, it had a full-size washer and dryer—and there was one large window with a spectacular view of the walking path below and the lake. There was no deck, though, which felt constraining.

My mind raced with thoughts and questions. It was too small, I might feel claustrophobic, I needed to be able to go outside, there was no storage, what if I had people over...and on and on. Yet, I couldn't afford anything larger—heck, I really couldn't afford this, as I was still paying a mortgage and maintenance on our family house, and I had a child in college.

I politely thanked Katherine, told her I would think about it and get back to her as soon as possible. I spent the next twenty-four hours weighing the pros and cons. Rental property was tight in that market. I had looked at other places online that were further away, where I could rent something bigger, but they had fewer amenities and felt less secure. My final thought was that I could live there for a year, if I had to.

I then quickly pulled up the website to complete the process. To my surprise, the unit was no longer available. Deflated and disappointed after making this monumental decision, I called Katherine. She apologized, and said that yes, someone else had rented the unit. There were no more studios available.

I hung up the phone, sadness settling over me. Then my cell rang; it was Katherine. She told me they had a small one bedroom coming up, which overlooked the courtyard instead of the lake, and had slightly more room with a balcony. It was also very close in price to the studio.

I ran out the door of my office, jumped in my car, and sped off to look at it. I arrived and once I had toured the apartment, I knew this would be my new home. The courtyard had a beautiful bubbling little stream that ran under the walkways and through the entire courtyard, and there were trees, bushes, and fragrant annual flowers everywhere. It felt right, like the stars had aligned, so I took it and began to plan my move.

Over the next couple of weeks, I began lining cabinets and gathering together the bare necessities. Even though I was overwhelmed at times, with feelings of loss and sadness regarding my separation, I also felt like a kid going to college for the first time. I had never lived on my own, and excitement and fear coursed through my veins.

Eventually, the day came when it was time to spend my first night in my tiny little new home. It really was tiny, so small it only had two windows in the entire place. My current partner, when he saw it years later, called it a storm shelter. Nonetheless, I was making it mine—in a meager way, but still mine. I slept on an air mattress for several weeks until I broke down and ordered a bed in a box on Amazon, along with a simple bedframe. Slowly, I was making it a refuge and a home very different from anything I had experienced in the past. This was a part of my growth, my therapy, and it felt almost like being on *Survivor*. Could I do it? Was I going to make it? Or was my codependency on others going to win?

As the holidays approached, I found myself sifting through clearance items at a big box hardware store, looking for Christmas decorations on a budget. I came across a large, three-foot-tall lighted reindeer, which from the box, appeared to be white and royal blue, with clear lights. What a find, I thought! I bought it, took it home, and carried the box out to my balcony. As I lifted the reindeer out of the box, there was an explosion of glitter, like a confetti cannon at a drag show! Then I felt a wave of shock and awe as I noticed that in addition to being covered in silver glitter, the reindeer was actually purple. No wonder it was on clearance!

I officially dubbed it my big, gay reindeer. If anyone living on the courtyard had a question about my sexuality, it seemed this would quickly answer the question. I plugged it in—it really was beautiful—and as the lights came on, a neighbor across from me and down one floor called out, "Hello! I love your reindeer!"

My face reddened, and I felt a tingling of warmth come over me. I might as well have draped a giant pride flag over my balcony. I was not totally out yet, so I felt a flush of embarrassment and fear, as I wondered what was going through her mind.

The neighbor was a sweet-looking woman in her sixties, with a salt-and-pepper bob and glasses. She kindly introduced herself as Marian and welcomed me to my new home.

Marian had a twinkle in her eye, a warm authentic smile, and a pep in her step—even though she used a cane, walker, and a scooter due to a disability. I soon learned Marian was a widow and had moved to the states from South America to be closer to family. She was well-read, highly intelligent, and an engaging conversationalist. She fascinated me and disarmed my defenses from the moment we met, and over the next few years, she would become one of my dearest friends and advocates—a friend, guide, teacher, and guardian angel, all wrapped into one. Bringing us together was one gift from my big, gay reindeer!

A few months later, I began to experience spring in the courtyard at my new home.

There was a ten- to twelve-foot tree growing and beginning to bud in front of my balcony, and one morning, while sitting outside, I noticed two beautiful cardinals sitting in the tree. Since the tree was still leafless, they were easy to spot, with their beautiful red feathers. They chirped at each other, they chirped at me, and then they flew off to a pine tree in the center of the courtyard area. From that day on, I always knew when they were near, by their common "pew, pew, pew" sound.

Cardinals tend to build their nests early, and, in this way, this couple was true to form. But they were building their nest right in front of my deck, in a tree that was not their typical choice for nesting—a pine tree.

Marian was fascinated by the cardinals' unusual choice.

I knew the birds were a sign.

My mother had passed less than a year ago and she loved, loved, loved cardinals. These welcoming, musical, heart-warming little birds were sent from her to comfort me, welcome me, and let me know everything was going to be alright. She was with me, for me, and was watching over me. The nesting birds and my storybook character neighbor were there to assist with my big transition to living on my own. I was not alone; I just did not fully realize that quite yet. The cardinals were sent to bring me comfort. My family would become larger and more diverse, with feathers, fur, and skin, than anything I had ever imagined.

This sign meant a lot to me, as I continued to move through a difficult time. I was still harboring a great deal of guilt and shame, still juggling relationships, as I tried to keep some semblance of relationship with my wife, and still not fully living my truth. My therapist, along with other friends and coaches, told me I would not begin to experience freedom and healing until I could live fully as myself and as a gay man. I was a bit confused by this, and I thought, haven't I done enough? How much more do I have to do? Also, I was so full of shame, guilt, and fear, I could not imagine ever being comfortable self-identifying as a gay man in public, let alone in a long-term relationship with another man. And I still wasn't fully certain what to do within my marriage.

Prior to my moving out on my own, my wife and I had sought support and reconciliation guidance through a national counseling group whose focus is on infidelity. At the time, my love for and desire to keep my relationship with my then wife was paramount. She asked if I would go on a retreat for several days for couples from across the country who were dealing with betrayal in their marriages. I had a lot of questions, was very skeptical, and felt unsure; however, after talking with the head of the organization, Roger, I decided to try it. Roger had assured me that while they were faith-based, they were not into reparative therapy to try to change gay people. He'd also said if my goal was to keep my relationship with my spouse intact, divorce or not, then this program would be beneficial to both of us. Sign me up, I thought! I bought plane tickets, made reservations, and off we went.

Truthfully, I still felt awkward and a little frightened, especially when I soon realized I was the only gay person there. A part of me wanted to keep my sexuality out of the conversation, but I had made an intention prior to going to the retreat that I would be honest, be truthful, and not hide behind vague words or descriptions. I'm proud to say I stuck to that.

In the group sessions, we had to share quite a bit, and this was one of the first times I got an inkling of what it felt like to be genuine, authentic, and real with everyone around me. It was worth the time, effort, and emotional stress, as I felt heard and seen. Maybe not accepted by all, but regardless, it was a valuable learning experience.

Through it, I also met someone who became instrumental in my life—a therapist who I believed really understood me, where I was at, and the opportunities, losses, and challenges I was facing in my life. His name was Ben.

Ben had degrees in theology and psychology and was also a sex therapist. I felt an instant connection and comfort with him that I had not experienced previously. He was wise, kind, and straightforward. He was disarming, with his calm nature, and yet, he did not shy away from the tough questions or presentation of the truth. I soon met his wife, Anne, who was also a therapist, and she was equally as talented, understanding, and insightful. They were the perfect storm for me—in a good way!

We began seeing Ben during the retreat and eventually he and Anne became our joint therapists. They were patient, kind, and thoughtful in their approach and treatment. Ben and Anne recognized my PTSD from my childhood traumas, the church, and from the bullying and rejection I'd experienced throughout my life. We had deep discussions about faith, relationships, and sexuality.

We talked a great deal about God, including my perceptions of Him, my misconceptions about going to hell, and my very rigid thinking surrounding God's grace, love, and forgiveness. I was having phone sessions with both of them, and I flew to their office a couple of times as well, to meet with them over a period of days.

There was something very special about the two of them. I could sense their love, nonjudgmental stance, compassion, and sincere desire to listen and gently guide me to my next step. I will never forget one turning point conversation we had in Anne's office, which held a warmth I could sense and even almost smell. I was sitting in one of the oversized chairs, and the three of us were discussing theology, and all the biblical verses that were used to shame gays back into the closet. The Old Testament in Leviticus. The New Testament in Romans.

Ben shared the original translations, and discussed how different interpretations had evolved over time. Then, came the kicker. He asked me, "What are the Ten Commandments?" After we discussed them, he asked me, "Which one says thou shalt not be gay?" His question was simple yet profound.

My jaw dropped, as I did not have an answer. "So, if, according to Jesus," he continued, "the greatest commandment is to love our neighbor as ourselves, and if you're going to take things literally, are you breaking this greatest of the commandants by being gay?" Then he addressed the worst-case scenario—which he made clear he and Anne did not believe—and said, "Hypothetically speaking, if God did not approve of being gay, would He vanquish you to hell based on your sexual orientation?"

My head was spinning as I thought through the repercussions of this possibility. It was an epiphany for me, as it was the first time I began to shift and think that maybe, just maybe, God still loved me in the midst of my gayness. Not only loved me, but wanted me to live my life to the fullest, with confidence, grace, and love. Home run for Ben! Because of his background in theology, he was getting through to me. I believed him.

Ben and Anne continued to help me after I made the move to my own place.

While at that point my wife and I were living separately, I was still struggling to move forward with the divorce. I was stuck and hemmed and hawed about it for years. I loved my wife and had tried desperately and unsuccessfully to salvage the relationship component of our marriage. The retreat we had gone on together was an incredible success, in that it led me to Ben and Anne, but it hadn't really helped my relationship with my wife. Things between us were complex and difficult. In addition to this emotional layer, there were practical issues, too. As part of the divorce, we would need to sell the home we'd raised our family in. It all felt heavy and overwhelming, as I carried the guilt, shame, and responsibility squarely on my back.

During one phone session with Anne and Ben, they were

talking with me about the next move for the two of us, and how to get unstuck. They knew how excruciating the divorce decision was for me; however, they also saw two people with intense pain, suffering together. After I said I didn't know if I could move forward with a divorce, Ben replied: "Sometimes, if you really love someone, the most loving and kind thing you can do is to let them go. Letting go is an act of love." This was another epiphany moment! The words from the messenger resonated in my soul and I knew he was right. I had to let go. I was making progress reconciling my faith and my sexuality, and also in growing toward more clarity of heart and mind around divorce. I knew, though, there were additional road-blocks in my daily life I needed to address. It was my first time living alone, and I was not doing it so well. Even though I was in therapy and growing, it was a process, and I was struggling to cope with my life and emotions. Sometimes, I would eat my emotions or drink them, all in an attempt to numb the pain, to not feel the intense pain of sadness, grief, and loss.

One night, after going out with my son and ex-wife for Father's Day, I over-indulged.

That night, something shifted in me, and I decided to stop the train.

I knew myself well enough to know that if I stayed on the train, it was going to wreck, and I did not want that to happen. I had come too far, and I wanted my adult kids to know I was a man of integrity, who would lead by example with love. I decided to totally stop drinking and surround myself with supportive friends and coaches. I also began to laser-focus on forgiving myself and others, loving myself and others, being honest with myself and others, living authentically, and serving others in my life.

It was all starting to come together for me.

I could not have a healthy relationship with God and others until I could have a healthy relationship with myself.

I began to feel a growing glimmer of hope. I was starting to like me.

Recently, someone in my life, who has observed me for over ten years, told me they have watched an amazing transformation take place in those years. "You are not the same man you were before," they said.

To that I say—thank God!

My first five years living on my own was a crash course in searching, growing, developing, and changing. My storm shelter was like my cocoon, from which I eventually emerged, and when I did, I was definitely more butterfly than caterpillar.

Reconstruction is hard work, and it takes time. And each of us has a different timetable for the process.

Holding our own journey and timetable with patient acceptance can be hard to do at times. When judging my progress or struggling with ongoing challenges, I find Chapter 3 of the book of Ecclesiastes from the Bible to be reassuring, in its confirmation that the timing in each of our journeys is perfect, individually, for all of us.

ECCLESIASTES 3:1 – 8, NEW LIVING TRANSLATION

For everything there is a season,
a time for every activity under heaven.
²A time to be born and a time to die.
A time to plant and a time to harvest.
³A time to kill and a time to heal.
A time to tear down and a time to build up.
⁴A time to cry and a time to laugh.
A time to grieve and a time to dance.

⁵A time to scatter stones and a time to gather stones.
   A time to embrace and a time to turn away.
⁶A time to search and a time to quit searching.
   A time to keep and a time to throw away.
⁷A time to tear and a time to mend.
   A time to be quiet and a time to speak.
⁸A time to love and a time to hate.
   A time for war and a time for peace.

During these deconstruction and reconstruction years, I at times felt I was walking in a desert, with no shoes, the sand burning my feet, the sun beating down and scorching my skin, confused, dazed, parched with thirst, and feeling lost. Any occasional mirage of an oasis quickly faded as I reached for it. Thankfully, I kept going, and I began to see the signs, the wonders, the guides, teachers, guardian angels, and yes—the timing.

CHAPTER 7

Teachers, Guides, and Guardian Angels

"When the student is ready the teacher will appear."

—Tao Te Ching

EARLIER IN MY LIFE, I do not know that I would have believed this famous quote, attributed to Lao Tzu. Or maybe it's that I simply wasn't aware of its truth. But now I see it reflected in my own journey. Once I opened my heart and mind to receiving, learning, and growing, I began to see these important people, places, and things that were showing up in my life. Looking back, I wonder how many missed opportunities, relationships, and lessons there may have been for me, if I had been more open and aware earlier. However, I was not ready, mentally, physically, or spiritually. Consequently, as they say, God is never late, and I know the timing of my journey happened just as it was meant to be. And for that, I am grateful.

I'd like to pause in sharing my unfolding story to reflect back on the patterns of grace I now see, which have emerged so clearly in the teachers who met me just when I was ready for them, or most needed them.

When I think about teachers, guides, and guardian angels, I think of the timeless movie *It's a Wonderful Life*. This classic has an enduring message. Don't we all have something in common with George Bailey? And at one time or another in our lives, we may ask the question, "What would the world have been like, if I had never been born?" During my dark night of the soul, I asked that question too many times. And then, a Clarence would show up. A messenger, a guardian angel, to speak truth and love into my life, giving me just enough to keep walking my path, one more step. Or, to help me come into contact with a thought or idea that had power to keep me going.

For me, I would think about my children and the impact my death would have on them. A child who loses a parent to suicide is more likely to die by suicide themselves, and it increases their risk of developing major psychiatric disorders.[2] This is a weighty fact. I once had a friend who told me after he became aware of it, it was the one thing that kept him from taking his own life.

The repercussions of our actions are profound and often unaltering. George Bailey was able to see, with his own eyes, the impact of his not being a part of this world, and then go back and reclaim his life and relationships. Seeing this helped him to not choose a permanent solution to his temporary pain. We do not have that same opportunity to witness, with

2 Harold S. Koplewicz, "Coping with a Parent's Suicide," Child Mind Institute, https://childmind.org/article/coping-with-a-parents -suicide/#full_article.

our eyes, what life would be like without us, but I believe that is why God, the Universe, sends messengers of other kinds onto our paths, to redirect us in our darkest hours.

A Million Little Things is a more contemporary television series that tackled the same thought line, albeit with a very different approach. The series started with a pivotal character, John, jumping to his death from his office balcony. He left behind a wife, two young children, and a host of close friends and coworkers, all caught in the wake of his suicide. Over several seasons, questions are asked and answered, and like in *It's a Wonderful Life*, we see and experience the ripple effect and impact his decision had on so many lives around him. I was enthralled by the series, often crying, as it wove an intricate pattern of John's life, his decisions, his impact, and the aftermath of his death. Like *It's a Wonderful Life*, the show shares the message that your life matters, it has value, and you have touched and impacted others in ways you may not know, or even see, on this side of life. Keep walking. Baby steps.

My angels and guides have also appeared through people coming into my life.

I've shared how my dear friend, Garret, connected me with his brother, David, at a critical moment in my life-and-death decision-making. Now, I know I was destined to be soul brothers with Garret. How do I know?

Since childhood, I have had a deep sense of intuition and vivid, colorful, and meaningful dreams. One such dream happened a few years before meeting Garret. In the dream, I was shaving in a locker-room-type bathroom, with mirrors on the wall in front of me, white sinks, and steam and humidity in the air. I could feel the terrycloth white towel wrapped around my waist. As I made a downward stroke through the shaving cream on my cheek, someone stepped up to the sink and mirror next to me. He was a ginger, a handsome guy, with the same white towel wrapped around his waist. As he turned, I noticed a tattoo on his upper arm, just below his shoulder. Then boom! I woke up.

I lay in bed, thinking what a strange dream it was. I had no idea who the man was, where we were, or what it meant.

I tucked the dream away in my mental filing cabinet.

Catapulting forward a few years, I then met Garret, a client, in the breakroom of his business, for the first time. I felt a sense of déjà vu, that I had met him previously and yet, knew I had not. As our friendship progressed, we eventually started attending a hot yoga class. The first evening, he took his shirt off in the locker room after class and I did a double take. Garret had a tattoo on his upper arm, and the image from my dream immediately pounced to the forefront of my mind. They were identical. In that moment, I really did not know what to think. My head was spinning. The realization later sank in that my dream had been a premonition of the future—and a friendship that would be a key component on my journey.

I'd also like to share more about Marian, my former neighbor. She still smiles and giggles when I tell her she is one of my guardian angels. I have absolutely no doubt that she is exactly that. She truly has a magical persona, full of light, love, and mystery, and seems to reach out at just the right time, by checking in, or sending a prayer or word of encouragement, or a funny GIF. I also tease her that she is like the Disney character, Snow White. Marian loves and attracts wildlife of all types to her courtyard apartment door. She adopted a feral cat and is known to feed and provide outdoor shelter to rabbits, possums, cats, and birds. She even names them all! Unafraid of her, they somehow want to congregate on her patio and stare in her sliding glass door, as if to say, "we are here!"

Marian is disarming, loving, and accepting. From the day I met her, with my big, gay reindeer, to today, I know she is a special, spiritual being, intentionally placed on my path to be my friend—but also to guide, encourage, and gently nudge me along on my path of reconciliation, healing, and living my truth. While she is not old enough to be my mother, I do believe my mother sent her, to support me in my grief of losing her, and to fill a void that made my heart ache. Marian has more than filled it.

As I reflect on my journey and the people along the way, I can see how my higher power sometimes placed friends, teachers, guides, and guardian angels in my life before I needed them or was ready to lean into them. I believe they entered my life earlier to gain trust, so when I needed to hear what they had to say, I was ready—and this is when they truly were able to show up as they were meant to be, from the beginning. Another dear friend, Tom, was destined to love and guide me on my journey of reconciliation and self-discovery. I met Tom in my therapy group. I will never forget when he showed up one day at my office, unannounced, with a cup of my favorite coffee, just to say "hello," and see how I was doing that week. He was kind and compassionate, and our friendship deepened over time as we caught movies, lunch, and coffees. He helped teach me what friendship meant. Tom listened, he was genuine and authentic, and he never seemed to want anything in return—just time and conversation.

I grew to love Tom and Garret, both as brothers and friends. One of my deepest desires was to have a brother, and now I had two! Little did I know, they were put in place, ready and waiting, to guide and support me in my dark night of the soul.

This dark night of the soul continued after we became friends. I still found myself with a sense of being at rock bottom, gasping for air, and seeing no way out, reaching for anything—alcohol, food, exercise—that would numb me, or bring some level of deflection and relief. None of it was a real solution, only a temporary balm for a gaping open wound of emotional pain and turmoil. I knew I could not go on this way, and I also had enough awareness by then to not want to end my life. The morning after over-indulging on that fateful Father's Day, overcome with nausea and a pounding headache, and overwhelmed with sadness, anxiety, desperation, and fear, I reached out to Tom and Garret. I cried, no, I sobbed, "I need help. I cannot keep doing this to myself." Like true brothers, they were there, immediately, and they stood by me, as they still do today. They connected me with a support group for people with addictive behaviors, which helped support me, guide me, and encourage me in making better decisions while loving and valuing myself. Soon, I realized there were many other pieces on the chessboard of my life, other people who suddenly came forward to share similar life experiences, acceptance, and love. They had been there all along, just like Tom and Garret, waiting patiently, until one day, *boom*, it was time to show up for something—for someone, *me*. They were each destined to impact me with their wisdom, love, and guidance.

Another miraculous interaction happened at this same time. Years earlier, I had a client, Rick, whom my company supported on a project. The project had wrapped up and I had not seen or talked with him for a long time. Within a week or two of my reaching out to Tom and Garret, Rick called about something regarding our former business interaction and asked to meet for coffee. He was someone I respected, admired, and trusted in the community. We'd had some deep conversations while working together, and my intuition told me that he would understand me, have compassion and empathy for me, and perhaps help guide me on my journey. Especially as Rick had previously shared about some of the major challenges and obstacles he had faced in his own life and business.

The morning we met, the coffee shop was bustling, with every table full. The buzz of conversation and smell of the steaming expresso brewing surrounded us, and I loved the energy, scents, and activity. Rick and I began by discussing all the related business items first. Then our conversation took a turn. As it became more personal, and as we leaned across the table, I sensed his friendship and noticed the depth of his brown eyes. I felt I could dive into them, like a dark warm pool, enveloped in acceptance and love. As my heart raced, and perspiration formed on my forehead, I launched into my current state of being.

How could I be telling someone I barely knew what a train wreck I felt like? I was supposed to keep it together, be poised, be perfect, be the one that others came to, not the one who needed the help. But in that moment, I knew this was my time of vulnerability. This teacher had showed up, and I knew it, knew it in the depths of my soul, that I was ready. He committed to being there for me, to walking the path with me, as a friend, mentor, and guide. In many ways, like Garret and his brother, Rick saved my life, too. In him, I found comfort, hope, love, acceptance, and accountability, from a genuine, authentic, kind, wise, and loving soul. I am happy to say that he is still walking with me today, speaking into my life at opportune times, always picking up my call when I need encouragement, input, or just someone to talk to or bounce something off. His background in yoga and meditation, along with his wisdom, truly make him a Master Yoda in my life.

Rick helped build my confidence and self-worth, so I was able to put myself out there, and even think about going on a date with someone. I am forever grateful for his loving nudges, guidance, and big pushes when needed. All of the preparation from this teacher put my heart and mind in a place to be open when Don walked into my life four years ago. Had Rick, the teacher, not shown up, had I not been ready as the student, I would have missed out on meeting the beautiful soul who is now my partner.

A year or so into our relationship, Don and I decided to search for a church to attend together.

I had become discouraged with finding a faith community that was inclusive and had diverse representation. Then, one Sunday, Don and I visited a church known for being somewhat diverse and inclusive. We soon discovered the church was going through a great deal of turmoil and transition; however, they had an interim pastor. When Pastor Tricia stood to speak, I was immediately captivated by her presence, command of the room, and the bright twinkle in her eyes. This was a predominantly older, white congregation, and she was an incredibly vibrant, black female pastor. She stood out in the room, for positive reasons. While she wore vestments, the fact that she also wore rhinestone heels, beautiful bangle bracelets, and unique and impeccably painted nails, made her even more intriguing in this inclusive and yet conservative environment.

As she delivered her message, she did not use notes; everything flowed perfectly from her heart and head. Her theological depth was apparent, as well as her ability to relate teachings and traditions of the Bible and church to an inclusive and progressive church body. I could not believe it. I had never heard anyone speak like her before, with such knowledge, passion, courage, and love.

Following the service, we made our way through the sunny glass lobby, humming with people and activity, toward the exit. Pastor Tricia was standing just inside the door, greeting each person as they exited the building. We shook her hand, she welcomed us, asked if we were new, and then handed me her business card while saying, "Call or email me, as I would love to have coffee with the two of you and get to know you better." I was not expecting that! I was also jaded from my past experiences, and on the way out, I turned to Don and said, "She probably says that to everyone." Nonetheless, I kept her card on my desk and looked at it for the next few weeks, wondering if she was truly genuine and for real. I reluctantly decided to send her an email, still thinking she would not respond. Lo and behold, she did! And before I knew it, we were driving to meet her at Starbucks on a Saturday afternoon, for coffee. A two-and-a-half-hour coffee!

Pastor Tricia was as lovely, vibrant, authentic, and engaging in person as she was standing in front of the church. She had an uncanny ability to look across the table into my eyes and truly listen. It turned out she had a gay son. Imagine that! She asked each of us about our stories and our journey, personally, with God, and with the church. She talked about the Bible, the relevancy of it, the verses used to shame the LGBTQ+ community, and contextually how the verses were written, and the original intent and translations. As she spoke, I kept thinking how I would have loved to take a college class from this teacher. Pastor Tricia's brilliance, compassion, and empathy quickly touched my heart and mind.

She was the real deal.

Pastor Tricia became a dear friend, as well as our pastor and teacher. She understood me, saw me, heard me, accepted me, and expressed a genuine love and concern for me. Something I had not felt in the church for a very, very long time. If ever.

I told her that she restored my faith in God.

After meeting her, I had a renewed sense of belonging and desire to be back in a faith community, one that expressed the love of God for all people—no exclusions.

Every Sunday, I could not wait to be in church. Her messages brought tears to my eyes and inspired me to take action in some ways. My relationship with God and the church evolved in this space; I no longer felt shame walking into a church and being me.

Unfortunately, Pastor Tricia's time was cut short at the church, and she moved on to her next calling. I still believe she was there for me.

One day, on the other side, I believe she will know what a dramatic impact she had on my life. I am forever grateful, as I needed that piece of me to be healed. This period helped me to believe again in a God who loves each of us, just as we are. And it showed me there are faith communities committed to inclusivity, while still following the traditions and teachings of the church.

A quote from pastor and author Adam Hamilton's book, *Seeing Gray in a World of Black and White,* summarizes what Pastor Tricia and my previous counselors taught me: "The ideal is that your faith not be rigid and unpliable, but instead that it is capable of being stretched and remolded over time, and that your theological and spiritual life grows deeper and more mature, with the passing years." Again, when I was ready, the teacher showed up, and I learned, grew, and changed. In reconciling my relationship with God and the church with my growing embrace of who I was, myself, I found a whole new level of acceptance and understanding within me.

I have learned much from the teachers, guides, and guardian angels on my journey so far, and I know there are more to come. I cannot wait.

I love the metaphor of the snake constantly shedding its skin, or the bird molting its feathers. Both animals cleanse, renew, and constantly evolve, never becoming stagnant. I can now relate.

My journey has taught me deep lessons about love and acceptance. Opening myself to others; having a willingness to learn, change, and grow; and unconditionally accepting others into my life and path; were all critical to my evolution as I shed rigid thought patterns, old habits, rule-following, and embraced a "what's next?" mentality.

It has taken me almost a lifetime to realize there are no coincidences. Yet, now I am certain of it. As I have been open, willing, teachable, and desirous of what's next, the teachers, guides, and angels I needed have shown up on my path. Sometimes, there are trolls under the bridge; however, there will always be someone to comfort, guide, and nudge me in the right direction, if only I am aware and willing. Some of the trolls in my life have been people and losses, while other trolls are self-inflicted negative self-talk, and reverting to old ways of thinking or patterns of behavior—self sabotage, if you will. But in the end, I am learning, as another treasured teacher, the writer Mark Nepo, so eloquently stated, that if I can accept and love others, and I can experience self-love and acceptance from others, we will all sprout up and flourish like grass.

CHAPTER 8

The Kaleidoscope of Loss

REFLECTING ON MY LIFE, I now see how it has been shaped deeply by losses, major losses. In my youth, there were a number of them, with the most significant being the loss of the presence of my mom, during and after her mental health crisis.

Then in high school, I also experienced the loss of a close friendship with my best friend, which impacted me deeply.

I had fallen in love with theater in sixth grade, around the time of my mom's institutionalization, discovering that the stage allowed me to express myself, express my emotions, and be someone other than myself. The applause was a nice validation as well. In high school, theater was my safe haven, a place I could escape the bullying, peer pressure, and be with other people like me. My best friend, Josh, and I were in several shows together. He was like a brother. I was not sexually attracted to him, but I loved him. Yet the bullying, taunting, and pressure from home around our relationship became too much for him. One day we were sitting in the tech/light booth talking. I could tell he was uncomfortable as he fidgeted in his chair, his eyes darting back and forth under his shaggy brown hair. He blurted out, "I can't be in any more shows with you. People think we're gay—you and me—and I just can't do it anymore. I am only going to do lighting." My stomach sank, and tears welled up in my eyes. It was not long after this interaction that he backed away from our friendship and theater altogether, as the pressure from his parents and peers was crushing him. I could see it. The loss of my best high school friend is still something that makes my heart ache today. He was doing what he had to do to survive high school and home. And I lost a brother, a chosen family member. In response, I pulled deeper within and eventually, temporarily, dropped out of theater as well.

The years passed, and I stepped into my adult life, experiencing more, smaller losses along the way. Then, during my period of deep alchemy and transformation, I received a phone call before I moved out of my home with my wife, one that began a cascade of significant and painful losses.

I was at work when the sound of my cell phone vibrating on my desk broke the focus of my attention as I composed a client email. I glanced down, distractedly, and noticed it was my dad calling. Interesting, I thought, as he rarely called me during the day while I was at work. He held a mindset he'd learned in a factory as a machinist—you are at work to work, cell phones did not exist, so whatever happened at home would just have to wait until you got back there. Knowing that, a sense of adrenaline and alarm rushed through my body and mind. I quickly grabbed the phone and answered it.

As soon as I said hello, he responded, "Kevin, it's about your mom." He told me they had been in the car when she began slurring her speech and then slumped to the side. He drove her to the hospital emergency room, and they immediately whisked her back to the treatment room. Could I come?

I was still talking to him as I ran out the door into the parking lot. I don't remember what I said, or anything about the drive to the hospital. Thoughts raced through my mind. Was it a stroke, a heart attack? Was she alive or was she dead?

Thankfully, the hospital was only a few miles away. With panic surging through my veins, I rushed inside to the front desk of the emergency room. When I told the nurse who I was, she immediately escorted me to a private room where my dad was sitting. He had bloodshot eyes and was wringing his hands as he told me that my mother had major heart failure but was still alive. He was waiting for the cardiologist to come back and talk with him. Soon my sister arrived, and we sat together in the room, with an impending sense of doom and dread. I had an inkling from the environment and the medical staff's words and expressions, that this was the gravest of moments.

I had lost my mother once to mental illness, unable to rescue her or help her in the way I wanted to, or had hoped for, during her lifetime. This incapacitating insecurity and fear plagued me from childhood to adulthood, in part through my recurring nightmares of her screaming for me to help her. I would always wake before there was any final resolution or rescue.

Now, all those feelings came crashing in on me like a tidal wave. Only this time, a voice kept telling me to be strong and take care of her (and my dad). Somehow, my survival instinct kicked into gear as the doctor, nurse, and chaplain approached me for a private conversation. They said my mother had suffered massive heart failure, and she would never recover. They could barely keep her heart beating, having brought her back to a breathing state with a ventilator several times already. There was no hope for recovery, and I believe they kept her alive until my sister and I could get there to be with our dad, as he had to make the toughest decision of his life.

My dad was beside himself with shock, sadness, and grief, and could not make the decision to take her off the breathing tube. The doctor and chaplain asked me to go back alone with them to see her and then explain to him the gravity of her condition.

I walked with them to see her.

The room she was in was sterile and full of bright lights. It smelled like death, and was silent, beyond the hum and whoosh of the breathing tube machine.

The moment I entered and saw her, I knew her spirit had already left her body. She was gone. Overcome with grief, I held her hand, and through the tears told her how much I loved her.

When I returned to my dad, I explained her state to him, and he eventually agreed she should suffer no more, and the breathing tube should be removed.

We were all ushered into her room and surrounded her bed. We held her hands, hugged her, and expressed our love to her as she took her final breath on that dark, dismal, rainy February afternoon.

I will never forget that experience, nor the weird dichotomy I felt in it.

I felt incredible heaviness at the loss of my mother's life. Regret, over unspoken words, unanswered questions, the time that could have been spent together more, the extra hugs that could have been exchanged. It happened too fast, too soon, too unexpectedly. I was not prepared, had no time for goodbyes or amends. Like a rainbow in my life, she had come and gone.

I also felt the freedom of the release of her spirit; knowing she was now whole, healed, and on the other side, with my beloved grandfather and grandmother. And I somehow knew they were with me, and always would be, until my time came to join them.

When I lost my mother, little did I know this event would be the onset of a series of further losses. The kaleidoscope would keep turning, with new shapes, sizes, and colors of loss weaving into the tapestry of my life.

Nine months after my mother's death, I moved out on my own and began to mourn the loss of a long-term marriage. I had always admired my ex-wife for her strength and stick-to-itiveness, as she knew exactly what she wanted from a marriage and a relationship, and she was not going to bend. I knew I could not deliver on many of those things, so in some ways her strength gave me the courage to stand on my convictions as well. It was not an easy process—divorce never is—and the pain of the loss still stings, and probably always will. It represented the death of so many things—the relationship as I knew it, our dreams of growing old together, the idea of a perfect family, the family unit the children knew, church and religion as I had known it, relationships with extended family, and many friends.

In many ways, I think divorce is a more complicated loss than a death. It is far-reaching and ongoing. Eventually new life comes, though. And for that new growth to take root, something must first die to make room. Yet, hearing that, or even knowing that, does not help much when you are in the midst of it. You must live through it, and I could not have done it without being surrounded by people who loved and supported me unconditionally. Also, I had to come to a place of acceptance. Acceptance of myself, my situation, my ex-wife, and my sexuality. Until I came into full acceptance, I could not continue, so a new life could begin to sprout for me. The longer I tried to bargain for something different, to fight with myself and God, the longer it took me to find peace. Peace comes through acceptance, and acceptance comes through loving myself and loving others.

As I made my way through these losses, navigating and often floundering in my new solo life, one of my apartment neighbors, Richie, died by suicide.

My angel neighbor, Marian, called Richie a sprite, as he was full of life and energy. I used to watch him stand on a paddle board, with his dog, in the lake by our community, and I was mesmerized by his skill and talent. Although I did not know him well, I ran into him often. He was engaging, kind, and talkative. Needless to say, we were all shocked by the turn of events. I attended the funeral with my neighbors, and I could not shake the nagging question: was there something I could have done to stop it? I had so many questions, and so few answers. I had regret over not having more conversations with him, not inviting him over for dinner. I know it's all part of survivor's guilt, and the need to accept the situation and not take responsibility for it. It also made me think about myself, if that was my destiny, and if so, the potential impact it would have on others. Also, seeing and talking with Richie's family, I witnessed the devastation, loss, and overwhelming grief they felt. This experience was another turn of the kaleidoscope.

My first few years of living on my own, I grappled with these losses as I also worked to find self-acceptance and self-love. After several years of living on my own, working on my health, healing, and recovery, and experiencing the gifts of my angels, teachers, and guides, my divorce was finalized, and I began living and accepting myself more fully. I was living my life fully as a gay man, and in a beautiful relationship with my partner, Don. The kaleidoscope that had shaped so much for me had also stilled. Little did I know this honeymoon period would not last too long, as another unexpected loss was looming on the horizon.

My dad has always been a central and pivotal figure in my life. There were so many good qualities about him, like his honesty, integrity, work ethic, thoughtfulness, and farmer's love for the land. I knew, though, I was different from an early age. I was more creative, did not excel at sports (although I tried), and I was very sensitive, prone to crying easily. But being the only son, I tried hard to be the son I thought he wanted me to be. I craved love and nurturing. My dad showed it in nonverbal ways, while my mother expressed it more verbally.

He was proud of his family and loved my ex-wife and our children. He was also very conservative, and the idea of his son being gay did not sit very well with him. I told him in my early twenties; however, he knew I was wrestling with religion and doing my best to stay committed to my wife and family. Needless to say, when my wife and I separated, he was sad and disappointed. It created a distance and a chasm between us that I could not seem to cross. I tried. We talked about it many times, but it was beyond his realm of experience and understanding. I wanted, hoped, and prayed, that one day we would be reconciled and come to a place of mutual acceptance.

A couple of years ago, I bought a house, and Don and I moved into it. I never dreamed this would be a reality for me.

Don and I were so grateful and could not wait to have friends and family over to our home. I really wanted my dad to see the house, and to meet Don for the first time. We invited him, along with one of my sons who was in town, to Easter dinner and, to my extreme surprise, he accepted the invitation.

Initially, it was a bit awkward and stilted, but eventually my dad grew more comfortable and spent the entire afternoon with us. Don was determined to win him over with his knowledge of farming, and it appeared to work. I was very grateful for that afternoon. Although no words of acceptance were spoken, his mere presence, time, and conversation were the most meaningful gifts he could have given me. I grew up with this man, and I had learned how he expressed himself.

Less than two months later, it was my dad's ninety-first birthday, and my sister hosted a birthday dinner with extended family. I picked up his favorite pot roast, gravy, and mashed potatoes from a local restaurant he liked, and pulled into the driveway as he also arrived. When he got out of his car, he abruptly turned to me and said, in an angry voice, "Who are you?" I told him I was his son. After a pause, he then replied, "Oh, you changed your hair. I didn't recognize you." I had not changed my hair, so the whole interaction startled me, and I knew something was up.

His behavior was erratic, and he seemed off balance at times, throughout the evening. He ate as normal, though, enjoying dinner and his birthday cake and ice cream. As the evening drew to a close, I asked him if he was comfortable driving home, and he said no, he thought I should drive him. The next day, we took him to the doctor, and he was admitted to the hospital. This began seven weeks of a roller coaster that I only wished I could exit.

During my dad's first week in the hospital, on June 11th, over a thousand miles away, my precious first grandchild, Callum Huck, was born. Excitement does not begin to describe the myriad of emotions and exuberance we all experienced. His birth was a bright spot during a week that also included brain surgery for my dad, for a brain bleed from a fall that seemed to trigger many of the things we had noticed in his shifting memory and behavior.

Shortly after my grandson's birth, they noticed he had a breathing issue and whisked him off to the NICU. It would be one of the last times my daughter held her sweet baby boy without tubes and IV lines attached to his tiny, yet strong, little body. After being diagnosed with a congenital heart defect, he underwent multiple procedures and surgeries in attempt to mend his dysfunctional heart.

During this time, my dad would have two further brain surgeries, always signs of hope, followed by a descent into madness. Seven excruciating weeks passed, as the lives of two souls I loved would ebb and flow, eventually passing to the other side within four days of each other.

Nothing, and I mean nothing, could have prepared me for the magnitude of these losses. Due to the medical decision-making, I could not be with my grandson during this time. He was not allowed any outside visitors until the very end, and then, only for a few hours. My heart ached and broke as I desperately wanted to see him, touch him, and to comfort my daughter, as she experienced a loss no parent should have to go through.

I was meeting with a pastor, planning my dad's funeral, the day my grandson passed. I flew to be with my daughter and son-in-law as soon as possible, spiraling from one level of grief to a depth I could not have been prepared to feel.

My daughter was extremely strong, channeling her love, grief, and pain into becoming an advocate for congenital heart defect awareness, posting this on social media:

Callum was a brave heart warrior during his 55 days of life. In memory of him this Heart Month, I'll be sharing more of his story and my experience as a heart mom. Heart defects are the most common birth defect, impacting nearly 1 in 100 babies. Approximately 1 in 4 of those babies has a critical heart defect. Often, babies receive a prenatal congenital heart disease (CHD) diagnosis following their 20-week anatomy scan. This was not the case for Callum. His specific defects were not detectable on an ultrasound, and having no known risks in our family, we had no reason to pursue a closer look at his heart. When Callum was in the cardiac intensive care unit (CICU), many of the doctors and nurses looked at us wide eyed with sympathy when they learned we hadn't known about Callum's heart. We hadn't known our world would be turned upside-down when Callum was born. His care team assured us that the lack of a prenatal diagnosis did not disadvantage him in receiving the best care and treatment after his birth. Knowing that was the case, I've made peace with the fact that I didn't know. Not knowing allowed me to enjoy my pregnancy, the days when I could feel Callum kick inside of me. He wasn't immediately whisked away from me after birth, and Brady and I had some sweet moments with him. The day of his birth was our only time with him when he was free of tubes and lines.

As the year drew to a close, I often reflected on everything that happened. Such deep losses. Such profound grief. Losing two lives that had left indelible marks on my heart, mind, and values. I wanted to forget, and I wanted to remember. And just as I thought all the losses that could accumulate in one year had, another one hit in December. There was restructuring in my department and my job was eliminated, effective immediately. The news was delivered via a Zoom call, and I was numb.

I had been working since I was fourteen years old, and I had never lost or been laid off a job. This was a new experience for me, another sense of loss, in a different way.

My partner and I were planning a dinner party for twenty people, two days after the news. In hindsight, the distraction, planning, and preparation were the best medicine for me at the time. I was learning the importance of the saying "Be where your hands are"— another lesson on mindfulness. One of the things I realized is that many people do not know what to say when you experience the loss of a job, so they say nothing, or distance themselves from you. That is not helpful. Even if it feels awkward, a word of caring, encouragement, or support means so much when you feel you are alone. Doing something is always better than doing or saying nothing.

Loss was woven into my life from a young age, and the past ten years have held the most challenging losses of my life. When I look back, I see that I am not the same person I was a decade ago. I have evolved, grown, and actively made choices to build a better life. I am learning that loss has its place.

I am not always ready for it; however, when it happens, what I learn from it can be taken forward into my life in a new way.

A beautiful way I've witnessed my daughter and son-in-law do this is by encouraging everyone in their circle of influence to do an act of random kindness on what would have been their son's first birthday. Paying kindness forward, with others, and with ourselves. Because after all, we need each other.

Loss is inevitable. Loss comes in many forms. And I know I will have more. It is the gift, or the curse, that keeps on giving, depending how I look at it. It can shape me, and it can break me, all at the same time.

Loss leaves a big black hole, a void, that longs to be filled with something.

I am learning how, and what, I fill it with, is the key to growth on my journey.

We Are Family

"YOUR DAD WOULD HAVE been so embarrassed by you."

These are the words someone in my family spoke in response to my partner being with me at my dad's funeral. I was grateful for Don's strength, love, and emotional support at this time, along with my son's. Due to the tragic circumstances with my grandson, no one else from my immediate family could be present, and I was feeling very alone and vulnerable. My partner and my son were my whole family in that moment, and I was grateful for their presence.

I didn't appreciate the cruel words that didn't recognize the love behind Don's standing there with me. Yet, I'm thankful I didn't believe they were true.

I closed my eyes and visualized the conversation my father had with me one evening in the hospital. I was sitting with him, helping him with some chicken nuggets and french fries, and he was struggling with his fork. We settled on him using his fingers.

He began to eat, but then he became disoriented and almost comatose. The nurse pressed an alarm, and suddenly the room was filled with medical personnel and equipment. All indications were a possible stroke; however, he began to talk. He told me he was dying. He also said, "I love you, and I am proud of you."

That was the first time I'd heard those words spoken from him in my entire life.

I was stunned, overwhelmed with emotion—joy, grief, and panic—as they wheeled him away. Soon the chaplain came to see me, as they must have thought Dad was dying as well. Thankfully, he survived another day.

The words he spoke solidified that I was his family, he had not disowned me, he did not hate or despise me. While he did not understand me, I now know he really did love me, and I do not believe he was embarrassed by me.

In the past, I would have gotten lost in those harsh words, as the last thing I wanted was to be an embarrassment to anyone. But I am different today. I am stronger, more committed to living an authentic and genuine life.

I believe, now that my dad is on the other side, he understands more about me. I also think my dad's concerns may have stemmed more from wondering if other people would think he did something wrong to raise a gay son. So, ultimately it was more about him, than it was about me. One of my therapists suggested that perhaps my dad's reaction to me being gay was also his way of wanting to protect me, especially in childhood, as he somehow knew that life would be very rough for me. He loved me, and he wanted to protect me. That's what family does, right?

Ironically, I somewhat did the same thing to myself. I used my judgments and fears to keep me from getting to know the people who would eventually become more like family. I guess we are all afraid of the people, places, and things we don't know, or have no experience with. They trigger something inside us, a judgement, a fear, that has more of a truth in it for us than it does for them.

I used to have a crazy fear of drag queens. And I did not want anyone to think that, because I was gay, I was going to dress up in women's clothing and strut around on a stage. Why would anyone want to do that—and how could I possibly enjoy watching it? Words I heard in the past would whisper in my head. "They are making a mockery of women. They are sick and twisted." So, needless to say, when I was freshly separated, with one foot out and on a business trip, and I was invited to drag show at a renowned club, *no, no, no, no* was my response. I told them I didn't like drag shows, that they made me uncomfortable. The truth was that I was uncomfortable with myself, with being gay, with being in a gay bar, and another man comfortable enough to put on a dress and belt out a tune, made me want to run and hide. But after a lively debate, I agreed to watch one performer.

We entered the beautiful, theater-type bar, packed with people from all walks of life. An exquisite-looking Latino drag queen, in a blue sequined evening gown, took the stage and began singing (not lip-syncing) "How Will I Know?" the iconic song by Whitney Houston. I was mesmerized. First, because Whitney is my all-time favorite singer, and second, because the performer was amazing. I had never seen or heard someone like this before—she was talented, looked amazing, and performed like a star. And she was a drag queen. All my preconceived ideas and judgments were falling to the floor.

After her performance, my friend whispered in my ear that we could leave, as he didn't want me to be uncomfortable. My reply was, "Leave? Hell no, we're staying for the next one!" This began my newfound respect for who a drag queen is, can be, and for the time, dedication, and talent it requires. I think, in a way, this helped me be more accepting of myself, and of others. It was one more step on my path. And it reflects some of the questions of family I have grappled with.

Drag queens seem like an unconventional family. As you observe them, see them represented in the media, you sense a comradery, caring, mentoring, and sharp sarcasm (that can be quite entertaining). It seems they have learned to find their family members, choose them wisely, and keep them close.

This has been a challenging lesson for me to learn, as it had been drilled into me that my family was only my nuclear blood family—and you do not trust anyone else. Consequently, my issues with guilt, shame, trust, and insecurities held me back for a long time from developing meaningful and authentic relationships with others. Let alone thinking of anyone outside my immediate family as a family member. After all, I had not accepted myself for so long—how could I possibly accept someone else, and truly love them as family?

Accepting and allowing others into my life at such a deep level meant that I had to accept myself, and importantly, allow myself to be happy. I had long been overly concerned and attentive to making everyone else happy—but never myself. That began with giving myself permission to be happy, permission to enjoy things, and permission to spend time with the people I liked and wanted to be around. Building a wider family, and a deeper circle of authentic belonging. Letting go of the vestiges of my mask and taking responsibility for being me.

Many of the old circles of belonging I claimed, or fell into, were the result of my mask, or denying of who I was. For example, I used to be a Republican. Why? Because it seemed like the right thing to do. I was told it represented conservative religion, a good economy, and beautiful china in the White House. I could not have seriously defended or debated my decision to be one, beyond that I was a follower. Several years ago, I decided to change my affiliation to Independent. I was sitting in front of my monitor, changing this on the voter registration website. The action felt difficult. As I sat staring at the screen, my head began to hurt, my palms were sweaty, and as my anxiety increased, I actually had a bit of a panic attack as I carried out this short online task. Yet, once I hit submit, I felt a sense of relief and calm. Something this simple was a major milestone for me in owning my sense of identity and beginning to have my own voice.

I've also experienced a shift in how I understand and engage with my work family.

Work is a big part of our lives. It is always stated (well, pre-COVID, at least) that we spend more time with the people we work with than we do with our families at home. As many of us have returned to the office, this will be true again. Consequently, we need to choose wisely where we will spend so much time and energy, as our coworkers are another extension of our chosen family.

One of my first jobs, post-church, was in an incredible advertising agency. It was headquartered in New York and had a large presence where I lived. When I went to work there, a part of me felt like it was at home. The agency was filled with beautiful, smart, and highly creative people. Everyone looked like they just stepped off the runway. In addition, there were several openly gay people, and it was made clear it was a diverse and inclusive culture. I had a modern office, large windows on one wall, and glass windows overlooking the office area on the opposite side. While there, I was happy, energized, and brimming with excitement about this job and the company.

Orchids have always been a favorite flower of mine, and one day, while strolling through the nursery, I spotted a gorgeous and unusual orchid plant. It was a splurge, but I bought it for my desk. It was an expression of me, a small baby step toward revealing myself to others. One day, the general manager, who happened to look like Diane Keaton, came by my office on roller skates—her easy and fun way for her to make the rounds and touch base with the large team. She stopped in, touched the orchid, and commented on how pretty it was, and how much she admired a man who was in touch with his feminine side. At first, I was a bit taken back, and then I let it settle, and I thought how true her statement was. I began to sense, she gets me. It felt like a good place to be.

Like all families, though, work families have bullies too. I just was not expecting to meet one in this environment. This particular person seemed to smirk as she passed me in the hallways. When we interacted, her responses were terse and almost jeering. I now know this is a prime example of bullying without words. I could sense her disdain for me, and I did not understand what caused it to happen. My people-pleasing self, who was working overtime back then, went overboard and did cartwheels to get her to like me, to no avail. As the abuse continued, I began to wonder if I might turn a corner one day and find her fist squarely planted in my face—just because she could.

The icing on the cake happened one day as I stood in the printer room, waiting for a document to finish printing. I could hear laughter outside in the cubicles and could specifically hear her voice. Soon, I realized she was talking about me, making fun of me. I later found out she said she didn't like me because I was a pretty boy. Upon hearing her, I pulled up my big boy pants and walked into the middle of the conversation, awkwardly shutting it down. I am glad I was brave enough to do that; however, knowing what I know now, I should have reported the many incidents to Human Resources. I did tell supervisors, but I never filed a formal complaint. I was insecure, a bit fearful, and held on to that shame-based belief that maybe I did something to make this happen—that maybe somehow, I deserved it. How could someone not like me?! Twisted thinking! Accepting that prejudice, hatred, and bullying are present, even in seemingly good environments, has been a hard lesson for me. Regardless, learning to choose my work environment and work family wisely, and finding a place where I could begin to, ever so slightly, inch the toe of my authentic self out the door, was an important part of my journey.

It was several years later, and with another firm, where I stuck my toe in the water by coming out with my CEO and some coworkers. My ex-wife and I were going through a trial separation at the time, and I knew that I could not hide my roller coaster of emotions from those close to me at the office.

I was terrified to tell anyone, as I felt so much shame, fear, and the nagging sense I was doing something wrong. I made the leap when our team went to New York for an inspiration trip. One evening, we participated in an immersive dinner theater experience, and we were all a little loosened up from the libations and experience. After the performance, the theater transformed into a nightclub. The lights dimmed, the runway and stage lit up, and club music began to pulse loudly throughout the room. Shirtless male servers were soon making their way through the crowd, delivering drinks and adding to the party atmosphere. Soon, I found myself on the dance floor with our CEO, Margaret. Margaret was a fun, professional, and approachable person. She was enjoying every minute with her team, and she loved providing these few days as a source of team building, fun, and creative inspiration. We danced, talked, laughed, and I soon found myself talking with her about my separation. Then the fateful words jumped out of my mouth. "I'm gay," I said, simply.

Margaret was unphased, and with tears in her eyes, told me I was in a safe place, and everything was going to be okay. She assured me I was taking a step in the right direction of self-discovery and authenticity. Of course, I cried, too, and we ended the dance with a big hug.

I felt as if a thousand pounds had been lifted from my shoulders.

I had been honest, and I realized my fear of telling the truth was not justified, as I had been met with a loving, kind, understanding, and accepting response. It was an important step for me in getting comfortable having these conversations with others and owning my truth, so I could move forward.

While work family has different boundaries than friends and chosen family, they are an extension of our lives, and they are family, too. We need to know we are in a safe and inclusive environment, in order to bring our gifts, passions, and whole selves fully to the table.

All these steps were important on my pathway to living my truth, having a point of view, and speaking it, with confidence. The teachers, guides, and guardian angels I've met have pushed me to embrace others, as well as myself. Many of them I consider part of my family today. I am learning that my chosen family is equally important, and in some cases more important, than blood family.

My chosen family includes a broad range of friends, family, and coworkers who love and support me, as I likewise love and support them. It includes my brothers from another mother and my chosen sisters. It also includes my tribe of the LGBTQ+ community.

Groups of people are drawn together by adversity, persecution, prejudice, judgment, and hate. While it does not feel good to be looked down upon or treated "less than," I do understand the bond it creates within our community. I struggle at times, being lumped into a group label, as we are each as unique as a snowflake, and yet we have a common denominator that binds us together.

As my sense of family has grown and expanded, and as my life has taken me (and my children) in new directions, holidays have begun to look different. They no longer revolve around seeing and spending time with my parents. My children are a priority to me; however, with their different locations and independence, it is unfortunately not always feasible to spend holidays with them. Celebrating holidays requires forethought and planning, so I do not sit around and feel sorry for myself. Recently, Don, our dog, and I, took a very long road trip to spend the Fourth of July with one of my sons. It was one of the best holidays I have ever experienced. Why? Because it was spontaneous, adventurous, and fun, and I was with both chosen and blood family. Those three adjectives also describe qualities Don brought into my life. Qualities I admired and was attracted to when we first met. It seemed risky to me, but I knew I needed more spontaneity, adventure, and fun in my life. He took my hand, and showed me the way, as my newest family member and partner.

The year I lost my grandson, and my dad, was the first Christmas I spent without either of my parents or any of my children. And this was hard. I am learning that grief comes in waves, and usually when I least expect it.

Again, forethought, planning, and taking action, were important to keep me from sliding into self-pity and victim-hood. I did two things that December that helped. One, we planned a large dinner party at our house with some of my favorite chosen family members (giving me an opportunity to serve others), and two, we planned a spa trip after Christmas and over New Year's, for the two of us and the dog (giving an opportunity for self-care). Both of these gifts to myself were important in this time, especially as it came right on the heels of being laid off from my job.

Building a wider family of people who love and support me has been a slow process, and takes work, discipline, and acceptance. But it has been a beautiful process. I now have a lovely and diverse family, filled with amazing people who have been placed along my path and in my life. And it helps me remain committed to building a positive life, centered in acceptance and love, for myself and others.

CHAPTER 10

Breadcrumbs on the Path

RECENTLY, MY PARTNER DON and I were driving back from a trip to North Carolina. While driving through Kentucky, we picked up a radio program, where the host was asking for people to call in who had been in long-term marriages and left them due to their sexuality—or to call in if you knew someone who'd experienced this scenario. One caller was a woman talking about her brother, who had left a twenty-year marriage and two children after coming out. She was clearly struggling with it, and felt it had wreaked havoc on her, his family, his ex-wife, and his children. She said, "My brother loves his children, and he always said that he would give his life for his children...but he didn't. Giving his life would have meant staying in that marriage and not causing all the pain and suffering that he did." The program host asked her if she would rather her brother had died, versus coming out as gay. She replied, "Yes."

Her words hit me hard. Because I, too, would give my life for my children. Yet, I had come to a place where, if I stayed and didn't figure myself out, I was literally going to be giving my life, and they would no longer have me in their lives. Staying would have proven tragic and detrimental for all involved—and I may have taken steps to enact a permanent solution for a temporary time of pain and suffering. That is what the caller did not understand about her brother. We eventually get to the end of our ropes, after working hard to resolve things, twisting and contorting ourselves to make others, and God, too, happy—and at some point, we just can't do it anymore. That is why the saying about not judging someone until you've walked a mile in their shoes is so true. We never know what someone else is dealing with, has endured, or the state of their mental health.

The caller thought her brother sacrificing himself for his family and children was the best option. However, is it better to wear a mask and live a lie while sacrificing self-respect and authenticity? While divorce is never an easy option, will his (and my) children, as they age and mature, look back and have a sense of respect, and even admiration, for a father who spoke his truth, let go of hiding and secret-keeping, in exchange for self-acceptance and self-love? This, in turn, will have a ripple effect on everyone in the family. Will I eventually become a role model for speaking and living genuine truth in love? A father's love is purely expressed in this scenario, freely, and with no barriers. Even though the caller's brother's children may not understand, and some may not even fully accept his decisions, I do believe that, deep down inside, they will know that their father did what was right for him and for everyone in his life. He ultimately did not choose easy; he chose hard. He chose to be brave. This decision requires more of a person than anyone who has not gone through it can imagine or understand. Staying in this life, showing up and being committed to living, living authentically, was the hard decision. As I have shared, I am thankful enough people were placed in my life along the way to help me see and understand that I needed to stay, and I needed to be here. Not only for my children, but for others, and for myself, to complete my journey on this earth, and to have the impact I was intended to have during my lifetime.

I tried hiding for so many years. We often think that is the answer, but it is not.

After testing the waters of sharing the truth with some chosen coworkers on my trip to New York, I met another coworker and friend, Amy, for a drink at the Plaza Hotel.

What a grand place to be! We sat at the white, palatial bar, surrounded by magnificent windows, beautiful people, and large, overflowing, fresh flower arrangements that sent the soft floral scent of roses through the air. Classical piano music played in the background. We both ordered champagne cocktails, and it was not long before I shared with her the reason for my separation. To my surprise, her response was, "I already knew." She shared that her brother was gay, and she had seen so many gay married people choose to live a double life or remain closeted for the entirety of their lives. Here, I thought I was hiding it from her, and in fact, I was not. Sometimes, others see more than we realize. Sometimes, others, who we are afraid to tell, may be our allies, if only we take a chance and share our truth. Amy had been touched by someone in her life, her brother, with similar circumstances. And even though she came from a faith background as well, she understood and accepted me with open arms. If I hadn't taken the risk to share my truth with her, I would have missed out on the empathy, understanding, love, and support she wanted to give to me. Being a people pleaser, I worry about disappointing people and letting them down. I began to realize that sharing my big secret was harder on me than it was on others. It was not nearly the scary monster I thought it was to most people. Amy has become a lifelong friend and ally, and I am grateful for the conversation that started it in that grand lobby bar in New York City, several years ago. Her response to me made a difference at that early juncture in my journey.

While family dynamics have shifted and grown over the years, everything is not always perfect. My loved ones, in my chosen and blood family, have learned that I am doing my best to show up in an authentic and genuine way, even when it may be more challenging to do that.

As I bring my story to a close, I want to share a few things that have helped me on my path to self-discovery, authenticity, and taking that next step.

One of the things that always drew me toward a career in marketing and advertising was the necessity to learn and grow. I could never stagnate, as it is important to stay on top of trends, culture, and consumer behavior. The industry forced me to be a perpetual student, evolving, learning, and growing. I learned the same needs to be true for my personal and spiritual life. Yes, I need to live in the moment and accept the things in my life I cannot change; however, I can still focus on personal growth and development, and that I have done.

One of my Gallup Strengths is Input. I am a gatherer of information, facts, and research. In doing so, I open myself to greater possibilities, new ideas, pushing the boundaries of my heart and mind. Reading books, listening to podcasts, subscribing to relevant news feeds, and attending webinars, are just a few of the things I do to challenge myself to grow personally and professionally. I love people! Yes, they can be messy, cruel, and hard to understand at times—but, they can also be kind, intellectual, thought-provoking, and challenging. Meeting new people, engaging in conversation at dinners or events, and risking an occasional coffee meeting with an almost stranger, are all potential avenues to learning something new. Even though the saying is, "Birds of a feather flock together," I find it can be stimulating, if sometimes uncomfortable, to spend time with those who are different from me. I do not have to agree with someone to listen, hold space for them, and then, with security and love, state my opinion or point of view. I have learned that, rather than avoid conflict, I need to carefully embrace it, and learn from it, as it really does make me stronger and more confident. This has taken me a long time, since it involved being comfortable and secure enough with who I am. Conflict has been a great source of anxiety for me in the past, but now I can ascertain who is safe enough to have these difficult conversations with, and sometimes I need others who share my point of view to be in the room, too. Boundaries are an important part of growth. I never used to have them, but I have them today. There are people, even some family, that I must limit time with, because it is not a safe, supportive, and mutually expressive environment to be in. I've learned that boundaries are an important part of self-care and loving myself, no matter how challenging it may be to sometimes put them in place.

The term self-care may be overused at times, but it's essential to stability, authenticity, and balanced mental health. For me, self-care also includes yoga and meditation, which I began to explore very early in my journey. Learning to be mindful and present were challenges for me. And to be honest, my rigid beliefs were so deeply ingrained, that I had to come to terms with an underlying fear that yoga was evil, or something God did not approve of. (It sounds crazy, I know.) Consequently, the way I ventured into yoga was by first signing up for hot yoga classes. They were more of workout, after all, right? I found a friend, Tom, who was willing to go with me. He came from the same conservative background and shared the same concerns. We secretly hoped that no one from the church would spy us sneaking into a yoga class—God forbid! He eventually quit going, as the mental demons of judgment and black and white thinking proved to be too much for him at the time. But I kept going, ever focused on accomplishing all the poses and having a strenuous work out. I was intense, focused on perfection, getting it right, conquering the poses, and the workout, no matter what it took. For so long I missed the real point—of listening to my body, leaning into and learning from each pose. Over time, though, like the first streams of light breaking through the clouds at dawn, slow and steady enlightenment began to take place in my body and brain. I eventually tried some regular, flow and Hatha yoga classes. The concept of quietness, being present, letting go, and sinking into my body, all began to flow through me. The little, tiny streams of light ultimately led to a bigger river of awareness and peace.

I have also incorporated meditation and writing into my life and routine. And I listen to my body, now. I used to force myself to do things or push myself to keep going when I was sick, tired, or sad. I learned finally, after all these years, and thanks to yoga, meditation, and journaling, I can usually (though not always) stop, listen, and take care of myself accordingly. And at times when I cannot see it, someone close to me who loves me will step in and say, you need to hit pause and stop driving yourself so hard. I still get obsessed with thoughts or things at times, and I need to be put in a timeout!

Having someone close to me observe my behavior and step in is not something I have always welcomed in my life. Today, such accountability has become my friend. It has become a reversal of thought for me, a good thing and not a punishment.

I do not have to hide anymore, and being seen in real relationship with others means allowing others close to me the opportunity to speak into my life. Garet, and another dear friend and brother, Bob, have a daily text check-in with me. In this group text, we share our plan for the day, anything we need prayer or positive energy for, and something we are grateful for that day. I know they are my family, always there for me, and I know they would drop everything and come running if I need anything.

When left to our own devices, without accountability and positive relationships, we will self-destruct—and I almost did. When I was really struggling and at my lowest, I knew I needed others. I wanted to be honest and transparent. I just did not always know how to do it.

At one point, I wrote on a piece of paper, "Stop. Breathe. Call Pastor Carl (an old empathetic friend from the past). Call Garret. God loves you." I taped this sign on the back of the front door to my tiny apartment. It showed me that I needed accountability for my actions, that I wanted to let others in my life, and that I wanted to believe God truly loved me. Sometimes it helped, and sometimes it did not. Regardless, the sign stayed there until I eventually moved further down my path to a healthier place.

When I was in my dark night of the soul, I never thought I would see the light of day. It felt like an endless tunnel without lights. I thought my life was over and I would never recover.

Today, my life is very different. It is not perfect, and things do not always go my way; however, radical acceptance of who I am and what I want has helped me build a life living my truth.

I no longer walk in a room and feel the heaviness of guilt, shame, and fear. Generally, I can accept myself, those around me, and my situation, and move forward with peace, authenticity, and positivity.

Many years ago, when dark clouds were overshadowing my heart and mind, I had a dream.

I was standing in front of a church, speaking. I have no idea what I was sharing about, however, everyone was smiling, and it felt and looked positive. Even though I never thought I would speak in front of a church again, I tucked the dream away, writing it down in my journal. Amazingly enough, after all this time, last year I shared my story, my journey of hope, with a large church congregation. I was surprised when the pastors asked me and another person to share our stories as a wrap-up to a series on inclusion and Pride. Though I was terrified at first, eventually my thoughts settled, and I embraced this opportunity, knowing it was the beginning of a new path for me. A new door was opening. As I shared a synopsis of my journey reconciling my faith, mental health, and sexuality—the journey within these pages—I saw the smiles, nods, tears, and connection being made with the listeners. God's peace and healing were present.

In that moment, I knew to the deepest core of my being that God loved me, was proud of me, and had me right where I was supposed to be.

I struggled to hold back my tears.

Joy won out that day. Joy like I had not experienced in a very long time.

A new chapter had begun.

After the morning I shared my story at the church, Marian sent me a powerful message. She wrote, "Thank you so much for sharing yourself like that. You can't imagine how many others you have helped. Not only the LGBTQ+ community, but also divorced people and many others, who don't feel fully accepted because they have broken some traditional taboo of the church. You spoke so well. The new you is ultra-amazing. Thank God!"

Soon after, I received a text from my son on Father's Day, which included a copy of an Instagram post from journalist Ben Ditto. It read, "Happy Father's Day everyone. Here's to great male role models (whatever form they take). I am very grateful that my father encouraged us to do the things we really wanted to do in life and do them as well as we can. We never got told who we should be or what we should do as long as we were happy and healthy. But leading by example meant watching him work in a highly responsible job as a pilot, excelling as a captain and never slacking off while doing a job he loved. Showing people how to be is always more effective than telling them how to be."

My son then went on to say, "It made me think of you. Thank you for always empowering me to chase my dreams and for pushing me to be the best person that I can be while also accepting me in any way regardless. I love you."

Wow! Both messages were confirmations to me that all the blood, sweat, and tears from the past years were worth it. Both made me cry, filled me with joy, and filled me with gratitude for not taking a different or darker path on my journey. Again, everything may not be perfect. However, the "truth will set you free," and in my case, those I love are seeing me as an imperfect, perfectly flawed human being, slowly walking on a journey to living with truth and authenticity.

In closing, I want to share a revelation I had, as I recently had lunch with my current pastor following my Sunday sharing. Pastor Chloe is an intelligent, deeply theological, kind, and compassionate person. We met for lunch at a hole-in-the-wall taco restaurant. It seemed appropriate, two renegade souls in an off-the-beaten-path place, discussing coloring outside the lines and the BIG love God has for all of us. As we munched on homemade corn tortilla chips and salsa, we talked about my story, my sharing, my inability to let go of my belief in God—from the time I was a young boy until now.

I have always believed. It's not a choice. It's a knowing I have always had deep within my being. Many I have known have walked away from God, no reconciliation possible in their minds. But I could not. I had to hang on. I had to resolve it.

Pastor Chloe, her soft brown eyes gazing at me ever so gently, looked across the table, and said, "Kevin, you are like Jacob. You wrestled with God, and you would not let go, until He blessed you. And He has."

She continued to share from the book of Genesis, chapter 32, verse 24-28, which says, "Then Jacob was left alone, and a man wrestled with him until daybreak. And when he saw that he had not prevailed against him, he touched the socket of his thigh, so the socket of Jacob's thigh was dislocated while he wrestled with him. Then he said, 'Let me go, for the dawn is breaking.' But he said, 'I will not let you go unless you bless me.' So, he said to him, 'What is your name?' And he said, 'Jacob.' And he said, 'Your name shall no longer be Jacob, but Israel: for you have striven with God and with men and have prevailed.'"

Tears welled up in my eyes, as the truth of her words sank into my heart.

I had wrestled with God for years and never let go. At times, I felt so far away from God and wanted to give up, but I did not, as my belief was too strong. I learned to see God differently during my wrestling match, learning who He really is and how much I am loved and valued. I persevered, becoming weak, broken, and strong during the wrestling, and I learned real humility.

My belief in God is stronger today than ever before. I am also more dependent on God, realizing in surrender, there is freedom. Putting my pride and arrogance aside, I can focus on others, on being of service to others, showing love, kindness, and acceptance. Also, just like Jacob, I have a limp from my wrestling match with God. Mine is not as visible as his, but they are still deep battle scars. They are present, mentally and physically.

Today, I am a different man, and I am aware of my limitations and my weaknesses, often reminded of my need and desire to turn to my higher power. "...we are weak, but you are strong..." (1Corinthians 4:10). My stubbornness and perseverance have paid off. I am so grateful that I never let go.

In sharing my story, I have tried not to sugarcoat my journey in any way, shape, or form. I have experienced a great deal of loss, pain, and suffering over these years of alchemy and growth. Through this process, I have lost relationships with family members, friends, and former church friends. It has not been an easy road, and I am thankful I didn't know the magnitude of it all earlier in the process. I'm also thankful I didn't, and still don't, have to walk the road alone. That's why we have each other, and why a faith community has been so important to me. I have had to, and continue to, take it one day at a time.

Many years ago, I bought a black Kenneth Cole T-shirt that had printed in white letters, "Stand for Something or Step Aside." I know, now, that was my passive way of saying I wanted to stand up and stand for myself and my sexuality, but I didn't know how it could ever be possible. Now, I can say I am standing up for myself and what I believe, without guilt or shame. For the first time in my life, I can look in the mirror, and I like who I see. (Well, I would like to lose a little weight and be a little younger!) But I see a man who, yes, is gay, but that is just one facet of who he is. I see a man who deeply loves his family, God, and those in his life, and he is, daily, doing his best to live an honest, authentic, and genuine life. I have learned the real meaning of John 8:32: "the truth shall set you free."

While loss has cut deep inroads through the riverbed of my life, I have also learned the meaning of Psalm 30:5: "Weeping may last for the night. But a shout of joy comes in the morning." I have experienced the depth of sadness and loss, and now the joy has broken through, like the sun bursting from the clouds after a dark storm. Loss and grieving have their place, and as long as I allowed myself to keep moving, keep processing, joy truly came in the morning. This year, my daughter gave birth to another son, my second grandson. After nine long months of tests, waiting, praying and trusting, he arrived, beautiful and healthy.

It's as if he knew his parents, family, and friends had been through so much heartache. He broke through and entered our lives with pure joy, and his smile, laughter, and giggles are infectious. The little guy exudes healing and love. My FaceTime calls with him are a lifeline. I have emotions and feelings that I never knew existed. This little guy touches my soul, and he brings exuberance and joy to the party! And he will always know he has an older brother looking after him.

In addition, I am now in a job where I can show up every day and be my authentic self while working for a good cause, something bigger than me. I experience happiness and joy taking my partner to events and get-togethers. I am no longer hiding, lurking in the shadows, worrying and wondering what someone else will think. I have chosen to love and to live. To love myself, to love others, and to love those who have caused me pain. That's not saying I don't have boundaries, as I wrote about previously; I am saying that I am motivated by love, and I am choosing to respond with love and kindness, whenever and wherever possible. Because in the end, what we put out into the world is really what comes back to us, isn't it?

Whatever struggles you face in your own life, whether they look similar to mine or are entirely different, please do not lose hope, and never let go. Joy will come in the morning.

My intention in writing this raw account of my journey is to encourage and inspire you to take the next step in your own journey, whatever that may be; to move you forward in living your truth with joy.

Keep wrestling for what you know and believe in your heart. Because transformation takes time, and we often cannot see it happening. It has a cumulative effect. The butterfly analogy is often used when talking about transformation and change—and there is a dramatic metamorphosis happening inside the cocoon. Personally, though, I like the Cecropia Moth analogy. I was fascinated by the grandeur of these winged creatures as a child. The caterpillars are large, chubby green slugs with bright yellow nubs that look like warts across their back. Interesting, but far from lovely! After they spin their silky cocoon at the end of summer, the larvae are hidden deep within the protective walls for two seasons. Then they emerge in the spring, stunning, large, colorful, spotted silk moths. I would hunt for their cocoons and put them in a container in my room, keeping them until their rebirth cycle. Breathtaking creatures, with their five- to seven-inch wingspan, and furry little bodies—I loved them!

At that time, I didn't see the parallel to my own life. Maybe something in my subconscious knew, though, that these captivating insects and their process related to me. Good things can transpire and evolve in the darkness of struggling and shedding. The key is knowing when it's time to come out, acknowledge the change, embrace yourself and the world, and take flight. Hard work, pain, surrender, patience, rest, and perseverance come before rebirth.

We don't have to go through this process alone. In fact, we couldn't possibly, because we're never truly alone. Keep your eyes, ears, and heart open for the teachers, guides, and guardian angels sent along your path, because they are there if you are open and willing to see and hear them.

Keep putting one step in front of the other, even if they are tiny steps forward.

The old adage is "time heals." There is an element of truth to this saying. However, the reality is that we must also show up, and do the work to process our emotions, feelings, and traumas. We need to experience forgiveness for ourselves and extend forgiveness to others. We will never forget, but we can forgive. It's a step to freedom. Five years later, as I look back, I can't believe the healing that has taken place in my life and family. There are new relationships, with new birth, joy, and hope for today, and for the future. Keep moving, even when progress may not be blatantly obvious. Others may see it in you before you do.

Believe and trust in the unseen.

Good things will come to pass.

AFTERWORD

"Hope and fear cannot occupy the
same space. Invite one to stay."

—Maya Angelou

My life has brought me to some dark places, and, for a long time, I didn't know how I could possibly move through them. And I know I'm not alone.

There is currently a three-fold crisis happening in the world and our Western culture today that intersects with many of the individual challenges and upheavals I've experienced and shared in these pages.

The first area of crisis is the worsening state of our mental health. Negative mental health impacts were already on the rise, particularly among older white males, and then the pandemic ushered in a whole new level of struggle, along with growing mental health awareness and new staggering statistics. Some of these are stark.

According to the CDC, it is estimated that 20 percent of people aged fifty-five years or older experience some type of mental health concern, including anxiety, depression, and other co-occurring disorders.[3] On average, in 2022, there were 134 suicides per day.

And according to the American Foundation for Suicide Prevention (AFSP):

- The age-adjusted suicide rate in 2022 was 14.21 per 100,000 individuals.
- In 2022, men died by suicide 3.85 times more than women.
- White males accounted for 68.46% of suicide deaths in 2022.

The second area of crisis is within the church and around faith and religion. For the first time in history, more churches are closing versus opening. A new study from Lifeway Research suggests more Protestant churches closed in 2019 than opened—continuing a decades-long congregational slide that is only expected to accelerate.

The study, which analyzed church data from thirty-four Protestant denominations and groups, found that 4,500 churches closed in 2019, while about three thousand new congregations were started. The thirty-four Protestant denominations account for about 60 percent of U.S.-based Protestant denominations.

From the 1940s through the 1990s, church membership held steady at around seventy percent of the U.S. population. Membership has plummeted in the new millennium. The decline is largely driven by a surging population of "nones,"

---

3 "Suicide Among Adults, Age 55 and Older, 2021," National Center for Health Statistics, published November 2023, https://www.cdc.gov/nchs /products/databriefs/db483.htm.

or Americans who claim no religion, representing 21 percent of the country, as of 2021, according to Gallup.

Millennials are leaving organized religion at staggering rates, and nearly a third of the Millennial generation has already identified themselves as being religiously unaffiliated. Why? One reason is that they feel the church is too hypocritical, judgmental, inauthentic, exclusive, or political.

Organized religion is struggling to attract new demographics at the same time it's failing to retain many of the existing and longstanding attendees who previously attended out of loyalty. People want to see the church truly be love in action, showing love, acceptance, and support for all who enter its doors. What many churches say and what they do are often diametrically opposed.

When I think about authenticity in the church and finding a place to belong, a couple of things come to mind. Recently, I had a conversation with a new acquaintance who came from a similar faith-based background. He mentioned struggling to find a church to call home and, more importantly, losing the desire to even look for a very long time. He told me about the church he had attended a while back—how much he liked the music, the people, and the messages. But in a conversation with a church leader, it became clear that as a gay man living his truth, he was "welcome" in the church but not "accepted." Acceptance meant living in accordance with their interpretation of the Bible and sexuality.

This is the sad reality many of us must face. We are only welcome in the church if we bring the portion of ourselves they approve. It is difficult to rebound from religious rejection, but sometimes it can help us realize the deeper truth that God is love, and He is the ultimate judge, not people. Our higher power will make a way and a place for each of us, even if misguided souls act as roadblocks instead of bridges to love.

The best resource for finding an authentic and inclusive church family is word of mouth. Others have walked before us, searched, been shot and wounded, and eventually found their way home. Ask others in the LGBTQ+ community about their experiences, where they have found a place of belonging, and why it works for them. You can search inclusive churches online, make a list, and start visiting. Take a friend, so you are not alone. Schedule coffee with the pastor or a church leader and get to know them. Ask all your tough questions—theologically and otherwise.

The third area of crisis is that, while we've made huge progress as a country in beginning to address diversity, equity, inclusion, and belonging, we still have a long way to go.

Many LGBTQ+ individuals are still not comfortable coming out at work, and wrestle with the social dynamics of family, friends, and church. Some laws have been passed to protect us from discrimination and bullying; however, there is still more work to do. Gay marriage seemed solid until recent years, as the Supreme Court has been revisiting past rulings. This has caused an undercurrent of fear and insecurity in communities and individuals, which underpins many relationships and aspects of life in general.

LGBTQ+ individuals face obstacles in being fully accepted, sometimes by themselves, and often in the culture around us. Not every individual wants a faith home, but for those of us that do, the rejection in these spaces can be devastating. And, like the wider population, we have mental health struggles. These three crises have come together to especially put the LGBTQ+ population at risk of suicide. This is evidenced by the following heartbreaking statistical finds from The Trevor Project, found at www.TheTrevorProject.org:

- LGBTQ+ young people are more than four times as likely to attempt suicide than their peers. This is a flashing red light warning for growing awareness and action by all of us.
- At least one LGBTQ+ youth contemplates and attempts suicide every forty-five seconds— throughout all twenty-four hours each day.
- An astounding 41 percent—nearly half—of LGBTQ+ youth contemplated suicide in the past year. This includes half of the transgender and nonbinary youth.[4]

Suicide is a tragic outcome, and we need to hear these young people's cries for help. More resources are needed and change needs to happen!

I hope, if you are having suicidal thoughts, you know my heart is with you, and I implore you to believe things can get better. If you have close loved ones in your life, please let them know you're struggling. Reach out to resources that are available. Open your heart to ways of healing. Know there is a higher power who loves you more than you can imagine. And if you open your heart, you may one day begin to truly feel it.

In this book, I shared how I swam through, and survived, the Bermuda Triangle of a mental health crisis, my faith, and my sexuality. My desire is that, whether your journey includes

---

4 "Facts About Suicide Among LGBTQ+ People," The Trevor Project, published January 1, 2024, https://www.thetrevorproject.org/resources/article/facts-about-lgbtq-youth-suicide/.

being a part of the LGBTQ+ community or not, you will find tidbits of hope and encouragement for yourself, a loved one, a friend, or anyone along your path who may be stuck in the dark, unable to see the next step forward.

I thought I would be forever stuck in the dark. But then I began to awaken, and what had felt like irreconcilable, lifeless ashes in my life became the new ground, leading me into more self-acceptance and love than I had ever felt. This is the beauty of alchemy. What has wounded us, what feels broken, becomes a part of our deepest beauty.

Here's my hand. Please hold it as you begin your own path of discovery, learning, pain, growth, and transformation. One thing I have learned is we are not meant to travel our journey alone. I am grateful for the guides I have had along the way, and I hope you find a breadcrumb (or more) in my story that will encourage, uplift, and convince you to keep moving forward...even on the darkest of days.

RESOURCES

I've been a recipient of grace through many people, groups, and pieces of art. Here, I share some resources that might meet you, the reader, in a meaningful way.

ORGANIZATIONS

The Trevor Project
- Suicide prevention for LGBTQ+ young people.
- https://www.thetrevorproject.org

American Foundation for Suicide Prevention
- Learn about suicide, how you can prevent it, and resources for those affected.
- https://afsp.org
- Call or text 988 for the Suicide and Crisis Lifeline.

The Kim Foundation
- A supportive resource and compassionate voice for those touched by mental illness and suicide.
- https://thekimfoundation.org

Crisis Services and Helpline – Boys Town Hotline
- The hotline is staffed by counselors trained and accredited by the American Association of Suicidology.
- (800) 448 – 3000

Psychology Today Therapy Directory
- An extensive directory of therapists, psychologists, and counselors in your area.
- https://www.psychologytoday.com/us/therapists

Body Memory Recall (BMR)
- Freedom from Body Memory
- https://jonathantripodi.com

RIM Therapy
- The Rim Institute
- https://www.riminstitute.com

BOOKS

The Miracle of Mindfulness: An Introduction to the Practice of Meditation by Thich Nhat Hanh

God on a Harley: A Spiritual Fable by Joan Brady

The Velvet Rage: Overcoming the Pain of Growing Up in a Straight Man's World by Alan Downs, PhD

In the Shelter: Finding a Home in the World by Pádraig Ó Tuama

Untamed by Glennon Doyle

The Gifts of Imperfection: Let Go of Who You're Supposed to Be and Embrace Who You Are by Brené Brown, PhD, LMSW

WORKBOOK

DBT Skills Training: Handouts and Worksheets by Marsha M. Linehan
- To be utilized in conjunction with participation in a DBT (Dialectical Behavioral Therapy) group or individual therapy. Groups and therapists can be found in the *Psychology Today Directory of Therapists*.

MOVIES

Will and Harper
- Will Ferrell's good friend, Harper, comes out as a trans woman. A portrayal of transition, acceptance, and friendship.

Boy Erased
- Based on Garrard Conley's 2016 memoir and experience with conversion therapy.

Pray Away
- Ex-leaders and a survivor of conversion therapy share their stories.

PODCASTS

All There Is with Anderson Cooper
- About the people we lose, the people left behind, and how we can live on—with loss and with love.
- https://www.cnn.com/audio/podcasts/all-there-is -with-anderson-cooper

ACKNOWLEDGEMENTS

I quoted The Tao Te Ching earlier: "When the student is ready the teacher will appear." I am deeply grateful for the countless teachers who have showed up along my path on my journey. Many are mentioned within these pages; however, there are many who are not. Thank you to each one of you who saw me in my time of need, questioning, and searching, and offered a word of encouragement, a hug, or a listening ear. This book would not have happened without you.

In addition, thank you to my book coach, Stacy Ennis, editor, Robin Bethel, and publishing coach, Katya Fishman. I never dreamt I could put my story into words, and Stacy's expertise, guidance, process, and encouragement made it possible. Thank you for helping me break through the fear that has held me back in many areas of my life in the past. *Alchemy from Ashes* represents a much bigger coming out for me. It is a way of saying, "This is me!" This is who I am and how I got here. Complicated, messy, and beautiful, all at the same time. Robin, you are masterful with words, deeply spiritual, and a bright light shining in the universe. Katya, your gifts of administration and logistics are incredible. My memoir is a reality because of this team.

Thank you to my son, Ian, for designing the book cover. You are an amazing talent, and I am grateful for this meaningful gift. My partner, three children, and grandsons keep me going every day. I have experienced love, acceptance, forgiveness, and reconciliation through my relationships with you. You are a vital part of the healing tapestry of my life and journey.

Finally, a big thank you to my beta reader group. You know who you are! You are a part of my chosen family, and you helped make this possible, and better. Your love, support, honest input, critique, and encouragement to create something deep and purposeful had an impact. I love you, and thank you, for constantly reigniting my hope and passion.

THE ALCHEMY CONTINUES

KEVIN HUTCHISON IS A SPEAKER on the topics of coming out and the impact on marriage, family relationships, and living with authenticity and truth. In addition, he can address sensitive issues around mental health, suicide prevention, and intrafamily dynamics. He is also a guide in re-imagining and re-establishing a faith relationship after being wounded by the faith community or others.

Some resources are listed in this book; however, Kevin is happy to share and discuss additional resources regarding sexual identity, faith, and mental health.

You can contact him at AlchemyFromAshes.com for more information.

ABOUT THE AUTHOR

KEVIN HUTCHISON is a marketing professional and former pastor, whose talent and expertise have been leveraged in both profit and not-for-profit organizations. He has worked for national and global agencies, held tenure in communications with a midwestern mega-church, and has served on boards such as the American Marketing Association and RESPECT, an education-and theater-based anti-bullying nonprofit.

Speaking, writing, and coaching are his passions, along with his love for his family, dogs, and partner. He holds a deep belief in a higher power and an innate good within each of us that can be unleashed through unconditional love and acceptance.

www.ingramcontent.com/pod-product-compliance
Lightning Source LLC
Chambersburg PA
CBHW030920140626
46545CB00016B/2118